Learning ELK Stack

Build mesmerizing visualizations, and analytics from your logs and data using Elasticsearch, Logstash, and Kibana

Saurabh Chhajed

PUBLISHING

BIRMINGHAM - MUMBAI

Learning ELK Stack

First published: November 2015

Production reference: 1231115

Published by Packt Publishing Ltd.
Livery Place
35 Livery Street
Birmingham B3 2PB, UK.

ISBN 978-1-78588-715-4

www.packtpub.com

Credits

Author
Saurabh Chhajed

Reviewers
Isra El Isa
Anthony Lapenna
Blake Praharaj

Commissioning Editor
Veena Pagare

Acquisition Editors
Reshma Raman
Purav Motiwalla

Content Development Editor
Rashmi Suvarna

Technical Editor
Siddhesh Ghadi

Copy Editor
Priyanka Ravi

Project Coordinator
Milton Dsouza

Proofreader
Safis Editing

Indexer
Mariammal Chettiyar

Graphics
Disha Haria

Production Coordinator
Nilesh R. Mohite

Cover Work
Nilesh R. Mohite

About the Author

Saurabh Chhajed is a technologist with vast professional experience in building Enterprise applications that span across product and service industries. He has experience building some of the largest recommender engines using big data analytics and machine learning, and also enjoys acting as an evangelist for big data and NoSQL technologies. With his rich technical experience, Saurabh has helped some of the largest financial and industrial companies in USA build their large product suites and distributed applications from scratch. He shares his personal experiences with technology at `http://saurzcode.in`.

Saurabh has also reviewed books by Packt Publishing, *Apache Camel Essentials* and *Java EE 7 Development with NetBeans 8,* in the past.

I would like to thank my family, Krati, who supported and encouraged me in spite of all the time it took away from them. I would also like to thank all the technical reviewers and content editors without whom this book wouldn't have been possible.

About the Reviewers

Isra El Isa obtained her BSc in computer science from the University of Jordan in January 2014. After graduation, she spent a year working as a software engineer at Seclytics Security Co., Santa Clara, California, where she got to work with various technologies. Isra is currently employed by iHorizons Co., Amman, Jordan, as a software developer.

Anthony Lapenna made a transition to working on the OPS side after having followed a career in software development and is currently a system engineer at WorkIT. He's a huge fan of the automation and DEVOPS culture. He also loves to track the latest technologies and to participate in the open source ecosystem by writing technical articles and sharing his software.

Blake Praharaj is a software engineer who specializes in navigating the hectic start-up environment. He is currently employed at Core Informatics, creating data management solutions for scientists in multiple industries that rely on laboratory testing and effective data interpretation. As with any good developer, he is constantly learning and exploring new technologies!

I would like to thank my significant other for her support and understanding with the time it took to work on this book. I would also like to thank the entire Core Informatics team for their support of the time it took to learn this technology, especially Vico.

www.PacktPub.com

Support files, eBooks, discount offers, and more

For support files and downloads related to your book, please visit www.PacktPub.com.

Did you know that Packt offers eBook versions of every book published, with PDF and ePub files available? You can upgrade to the eBook version at www.PacktPub.com and as a print book customer, you are entitled to a discount on the eBook copy. Get in touch with us at service@packtpub.com for more details.

At www.PacktPub.com, you can also read a collection of free technical articles, sign up for a range of free newsletters and receive exclusive discounts and offers on Packt books and eBooks.

https://www2.packtpub.com/books/subscription/packtlib

Do you need instant solutions to your IT questions? PacktLib is Packt's online digital book library. Here, you can search, access, and read Packt's entire library of books.

Why subscribe?
- Fully searchable across every book published by Packt
- Copy and paste, print, and bookmark content
- On demand and accessible via a web browser

Free access for Packt account holders

If you have an account with Packt at www.PacktPub.com, you can use this to access PacktLib today and view 9 entirely free books. Simply use your login credentials for immediate access.

Table of Contents

Preface

This book is aimed at introducing the building of your own ELK Stack data pipeline using the open source technologies stack of Elasticsearch, Logstash, and Kibana. This book is also aimed at covering the core concepts of each of the components of the stack and quickly using them to build your own log analytics solutions. The book is divided into ten chapters. The first chapter helps you install all the components of the stack so that you can quickly build your first data pipeline in the second chapter. Chapter 3 to Chapter 7 introduce you to the capabilities of each of the components of the stack in detail. The eighth chapter builds a full data pipeline using ELK. The ninth chapter introduces you to some of the use cases of the ELK Stack in practice. Finally, the tenth chapter helps you know about some of the tools that can work with ELK Stack to enhance its capabilities.

What this book covers

Chapter 1, *Introduction to ELK Stack*, introduces ELK Stack, and what problems it solves for you. It explains the role of each component in the stack, and also gets you up and running with ELK Stack and with installations of all its components—Elasticsearch, Logstash, and Kibana.

Chapter 2, *Building Your First Data Pipeline with ELK*, helps you build a basic ELK Stack pipeline using a CSV formatted input, and explores the basic configurations to get your ELK Stack up and running to analyze data quickly.

Chapter 3, *Collect, Parse, and Transform Data with Logstash*, covers the key features of Logstash, and explains how Logstash helps integrate with a variety of input and output sources. This chapter also aims to explain various Logstash input, filter, and output plugins, which help collect, parse, transform, and ship data using Logstash.

Chapter 4, Creating Custom Logstash Plugins, explains how we can create our own custom Logstash plugins catering to our various needs that are not satisfied using the already available plugins. It explains the lifecycle of a `logstash` plugin and how various types of input, filter, and output plugins can be developed and published.

Chapter 5, Why Do We Need Elasticsearch in ELK?, explains the role of Elasticsearch in ELK Stack, and explains the key features and basics of Elasticsearch, such as index, documents, shards, clusters, and so on. It also covers various indexing and searching APIs and Query DSLs available in Elasticsearch.

Chapter 6, Finding Insights with Kibana, explains how to use Kibana to search, view, and interact in real time with data that is stored in the Elasticsearch indices. It explores the various search options that are available, and how we can use the **Discover** page of the Kibana interface.

Chapter 7, Kibana – Visualization and Dashboard, explains in detail about the various visualizations and dashboards that are available in Kibana with various examples. It also explains the **Settings** page, which helps configure the index patterns, scripted fields, and so on.

Chapter 8, Putting It All Together, shows the combination of all three components to build a fully-fledged data pipeline using ELK Stack, mentioning the role of each of the components as explained in previous chapters.

Chapter 9, ELK Stack in Production, explains some of the important points to keep in mind while using ELK Stack in production. It also explains the various use cases, and case studies that make use of ELK Stack in various use cases across the industry.

Chapter 10, Expanding Horizons with ELK, explains various tools, which combined with ELK, enhances the capabilities of the stack.

What you need for this book

- Unix Operating System (Any flavor)
- Elasticsearch 1.5.2
- Logstash 1.5.0
- Kibana 4.0.2

Who this book is for

This book is for anyone who wants to analyze data using low-cost options. No prior knowledge of ELK Stack or its components is expected, although familiarity with NoSQL databases and some programming knowledge will be helpful.

Conventions

In this book, you will find a number of text styles that distinguish between different kinds of information. Here are some examples of these styles, and an explanation of their meaning.

Code words in text, database table names, folder names, filenames, file extensions, pathnames, dummy URLs, user input, and Twitter handles are shown as follows: "The preceding command will install the `rabbitmq` input plugin to the Logstash installation."

A block of code is set as follows:

```
filter {
drop {
}
}
```

Any command-line input or output is written as follows:

```
$bin/plugin install logstash-input-rabbitmq
```

New terms and **important words** are shown in bold. Words that you see on the screen, for example, in menus or dialog boxes, appear in the text like this: "Clicking the **Next** button moves you to the next screen."

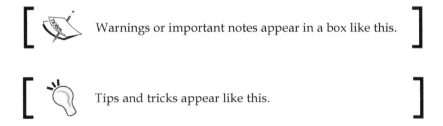

Warnings or important notes appear in a box like this.

Tips and tricks appear like this.

Reader feedback

Feedback from our readers is always welcome. Let us know what you think about this book—what you liked or disliked. Reader feedback is important for us as it helps us develop titles that you will really get the most out of.

To send us general feedback, simply e-mail `feedback@packtpub.com`, and mention the book's title in the subject of your message.

If there is a topic that you have expertise in and you are interested in either writing or contributing to a book, see our author guide at `www.packtpub.com/authors`.

Customer support

Now that you are the proud owner of a Packt book, we have a number of things to help you to get the most from your purchase.

Downloading the example code

You can download the example code files from your account at `http://www.packtpub.com` for all the Packt Publishing books you have purchased. If you purchased this book elsewhere, you can visit `http://www.packtpub.com/support` and register to have the files e-mailed directly to you.

Downloading the color images of this book

We also provide you with a PDF file that has color images of the screenshots/diagrams used in this book. The color images will help you better understand the changes in the output. You can download this file from `https://www.packtpub.com/sites/default/files/downloads/71540S_ColorImages.pdf`.

Errata

Although we have taken every care to ensure the accuracy of our content, mistakes do happen. If you find a mistake in one of our books—maybe a mistake in the text or the code—we would be grateful if you could report this to us. By doing so, you can save other readers from frustration and help us improve subsequent versions of this book. If you find any errata, please report them by visiting `http://www.packtpub.com/submit-errata`, selecting your book, clicking on the **Errata Submission Form** link, and entering the details of your errata. Once your errata are verified, your submission will be accepted and the errata will be uploaded to our website or added to any list of existing errata under the Errata section of that title.

To view the previously submitted errata, go to `https://www.packtpub.com/books/content/support` and enter the name of the book in the search field. The required information will appear under the **Errata** section.

Piracy

Piracy of copyrighted material on the Internet is an ongoing problem across all media. At Packt, we take the protection of our copyright and licenses very seriously. If you come across any illegal copies of our works in any form on the Internet, please provide us with the location address or website name immediately so that we can pursue a remedy.

Please contact us at `copyright@packtpub.com` with a link to the suspected pirated material.

We appreciate your help in protecting our authors and our ability to bring you valuable content.

Questions

If you have a problem with any aspect of this book, you can contact us at `questions@packtpub.com`, and we will do our best to address the problem.

1
Introduction to ELK Stack

This chapter explains the importance of log analysis in today's data-driven world and what are the challenges associated with log analysis. It introduces ELK stack as a complete log analysis solution, and explains what ELK stack is and the role of each of the open source components of the stack, namely, Elasticsearch, Logstash, and Kibana. Also, it briefly explains the key features of each of the components and describes the installation and configuration steps for them.

The need for log analysis

Logs provide us with necessary information on how our system is behaving. However, the content and format of the logs varies among different services or say, among different components of the same system. For example, a scanner may log error messages related to communication with other devices; on the other hand, a web server logs information on all incoming requests, outgoing responses, time taken for a response, and so on. Similarly, application logs for an e-commerce website will log business-specific logs.

As the logs vary by their content, so will their uses. For example, the logs from a scanner may be used for troubleshooting or for a simple status check or reporting while the web server log is used to analyze traffic patterns across multiple products. Analysis of logs from an e-commerce site can help figure out whether packages from a specific location are returned repeatedly and the probable reasons for the same.

The following are some common use cases where log analysis is helpful:

- Issue debugging
- Performance analysis
- Security analysis
- Predictive analysis
- **Internet of things** (IoT) and logging

Issue debugging

Debugging is one of the most common reasons to enable logging within your application. The simplest and most frequent use for a debug log is to grep for a specific error message or event occurrence. If a system administrator believes that a program crashed because of a network failure, then he or she will try to find a `connection dropped` message or a similar message in the server logs to analyze what caused the issue. Once the bug or the issue is identified, log analysis solutions help capture application information and snapshots of that particular time can be easily passed across development teams to analyze it further.

Performance analysis

Log analysis helps optimize or debug system performance and give essential inputs around bottlenecks in the system. Understanding a system's performance is often about understanding resource usage in the system. Logs can help analyze individual resource usage in the system, behavior of multiple threads in the application, potential deadlock conditions, and so on. Logs also carry with them timestamp information, which is essential to analyze how the system is behaving over time. For instance, a web server log can help know how individual services are performing based on response times, HTTP response codes, and so on.

Security analysis

Logs play a vital role in managing the application security for any organization. They are particularly helpful to detect security breaches, application misuse, malicious attacks, and so on. When users interact with the system, it generates log events, which can help track user behavior, identify suspicious activities, and raise alarms or security incidents for breaches.

The intrusion detection process involves session reconstruction from the logs itself. For example, `ssh` login events in the system can be used to identify any breaches on the machines.

Predictive analysis

Predictive analysis is one of the hot trends of recent times. Logs and events data can be used for very accurate predictive analysis. Predictive analysis models help in identifying potential customers, resource planning, inventory management and optimization, workload efficiency, and efficient resource scheduling. It also helps guide the marketing strategy, user-segment targeting, ad-placement strategy, and so on.

Internet of things and logging

When it comes to IoT devices (devices or machines that interact with each other without any human intervention), it is vital that the system is monitored and managed to keep downtime to a minimum and resolve any important bugs or issues swiftly. Since these devices should be able to work with little human intervention and may exist on a large geographical scale, log data is expected to play a crucial role in understanding system behavior and reducing downtime.

Challenges in log analysis

The current log analysis process mostly involves checking logs at multiple servers that are written by different components and systems across your application. This has various problems, which makes it a time-consuming and tedious job. Let's look at some of the common problem scenarios:

- Non-consistent log format
- Decentralized logs
- Expert knowledge requirement

Non-consistent log format

Every application and device logs in its own special way, so each format needs its own expert. Also, it is difficult to search across because of different formats.

Let's take a look at some of the common log formats. An interesting thing to observe will be the way different logs represent different timestamp formats, different ways to represent INFO, ERROR, and so on, and the order of these components with logs. It's difficult to figure out just by seeing logs what is present at what location. This is where tools such as Logstash help.

Tomcat logs

A typical tomcat server startup log entry will look like this:

```
May 24, 2015 3:56:26 PM org.apache.catalina.startup.HostConfig deployWAR
INFO: Deployment of web application archive \soft\apache-tomcat-7.0.62\
webapps\sample.war has finished in 253 ms
```

Apache access logs – combined log format

A typical Apache access log entry will look like this:

```
127.0.0.1 - - [24/May/2015:15:54:59 +0530] "GET /favicon.ico HTTP/1.1"
200 21630
```

IIS logs

A typical IIS log entry will look like this:

```
2012-05-02 17:42:15 172.24.255.255 - 172.20.255.255 80 GET /images/
favicon.ico - 200 Mozilla/4.0+(compatible;MSIE+5.5;+Windows+2000+Server)
```

Variety of time formats

Not only log formats, but timestamp formats are also different among different types of applications, different types of events generated across multiple devices, and so on. Different types of time formats across different components of your system also make it difficult to correlate events occurring across multiple systems at the same time:

- 142920788
- Oct 12 23:21:45
- [5/May/2015:08:09:10 +0000]
- Tue 01-01-2009 6:00
- 2015-05-30 T 05:45 UTC
- Sat Jul 23 02:16:57 2014
- 07:38, 11 December 2012 (UTC)

Decentralized logs

Logs are mostly spread across all the applications that may be across different servers and different components. The complexity of log analysis increases with multiple components logging at multiple locations. For one or two servers' setup, finding out some information from logs involves running `cat` or `tail` commands or piping these results to `grep` command. But what if you have `10`, `20`, or say, `100` servers? These kinds of searches are mostly not scalable for a huge cluster of machines and need a centralized log management and an analysis solution.

Expert knowledge requirement

People interested in getting the required business-centric information out of logs generally don't have access to the logs or may not have the technical expertise to figure out the appropriate information in the quickest possible way, which can make analysis slower, and sometimes, impossible too.

The ELK Stack

The ELK platform is a complete log analytics solution, built on a combination of three open source tools—Elasticsearch, Logstash, and Kibana. It tries to address all the problems and challenges that we saw in the previous section. ELK utilizes the open source stack of Elasticsearch for deep search and data analytics; Logstash for centralized logging management, which includes shipping and forwarding the logs from multiple servers, log enrichment, and parsing; and finally, Kibana for powerful and beautiful data visualizations. ELK stack is currently maintained and actively supported by the company called Elastic (formerly, Elasticsearch).

Let's look at a brief overview of each of these systems:

*   Elasticsearch
*   Logstash
*   Kibana

Elasticsearch

Elasticsearch is a distributed open source search engine based on Apache Lucene, and released under an Apache 2.0 license (which means that it can be downloaded, used, and modified free of charge). It provides horizontal scalability, reliability, and multitenant capability for real-time search. Elasticsearch features are available through JSON over a RESTful API. The searching capabilities are backed by a schema-less Apache Lucene Engine, which allows it to dynamically index data without knowing the structure beforehand. Elasticsearch is able to achieve fast search responses because it uses indexing to search over the texts.

Elasticsearch is used by many big companies, such as GitHub, SoundCloud, FourSquare, Netflix, and many others. Some of the use cases are as follows:

*   **Wikipedia**: This uses Elasticsearch to provide a full text search, and provide functionalities, such as *search-as-you-type*, and *did-you-mean* suggestions.

- **The Guardian**: This uses Elasticsearch to process 40 million documents per day, provide real-time analytics of site-traffic across the organization, and help understand audience engagement better.

- **StumbleUpon**: This uses Elasticsearch to power intelligent searches across its platform and provide great recommendations to millions of customers.

- **SoundCloud**: This uses Elasticsearch to provide real-time search capabilities for millions of users across geographies.

- **GitHub**: This uses Elasticsearch to index over 8 million code repositories, and index multiple events across the platform, hence providing real-time search capabilities across it.

Some of the key features of Elasticsearch are:

- It is an open source distributed, scalable, and highly available real-time document store

- It provides real-time search and analysis capabilities

- It provides a sophisticated RESTful API to play around with lookup, and various features, such as multilingual search, geolocation, autocomplete, contextual did-you-mean suggestions, and result snippets

- It can be scaled horizontally easily and provides easy integrations with cloud-based infrastructures, such as AWS and others

Logstash

Logstash is a data pipeline that helps collect, parse, and analyze a large variety of structured and unstructured data and events generated across various systems. It provides plugins to connect to various types of input sources and platforms, and is designed to efficiently process logs, events, and unstructured data sources for distribution into a variety of outputs with the use of its output plugins, namely file, stdout (as output on console running Logstash), or Elasticsearch.

It has the following key features:

- **Centralized data processing**: Logstash helps build a data pipeline that can centralize data processing. With the use of a variety of plugins for input and output, it can convert a lot of different input sources to a single common format.

- **Support for custom log formats**: Logs written by different applications often have particular formats specific to the application. Logstash helps parse and process custom formats on a large scale. It provides support to write your own filters for tokenization and also provides ready-to-use filters.

- **Plugin development**: Custom plugins can be developed and published, and there is a large variety of custom developed plugins already available.

Kibana

Kibana is an open source Apache 2.0 licensed data visualization platform that helps in visualizing any kind of structured and unstructured data stored in Elasticsearch indexes. Kibana is entirely written in HTML and JavaScript. It uses the powerful search and indexing capabilities of Elasticsearch exposed through its RESTful API to display powerful graphics for the end users. From basic business intelligence to real-time debugging, Kibana plays its role through exposing data through beautiful histograms, geomaps, pie charts, graphs, tables, and so on.

Kibana makes it easy to understand large volumes of data. Its simple browser-based interface enables you to quickly create and share dynamic dashboards that display changes to Elasticsearch queries in real time.

Some of the key features of Kibana are as follows:

- It provides flexible analytics and a visualization platform for business intelligence.

- It provides real-time analysis, summarization, charting, and debugging capabilities.

- It provides an intuitive and user friendly interface, which is highly customizable through some drag and drop features and alignments as and when needed.

- It allows saving the dashboard, and managing more than one dashboard. Dashboards can be easily shared and embedded within different systems.

- It allows sharing snapshots of logs that you have already searched through, and isolates multiple problem transactions.

ELK data pipeline

A typical ELK stack data pipeline looks something like this:

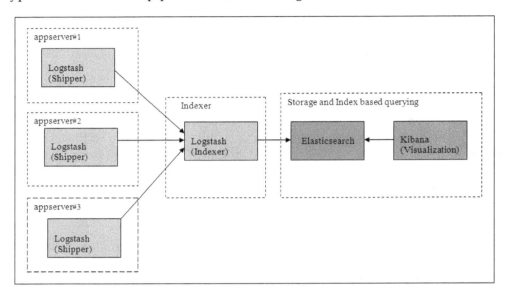

In a typical ELK Stack data pipeline, logs from multiple application servers are shipped through Logstash shipper to a centralized Logstash indexer. The Logstash indexer will output data to an Elasticsearch cluster, which will be queried by Kibana to display great visualizations and build dashboards over the log data.

ELK Stack installation

A Java runtime is required to run ELK Stack. The latest version of Java is recommended for the installation. At the time of writing this book, the minimum requirement is Java 7. You can use the official Oracle distribution, or an open source distribution, such as OpenJDK.

You can verify the Java installation by running the following command in your shell:

```
> java -version
java version "1.8.0_40"
Java(TM) SE Runtime Environment (build 1.8.0_40-b26)
Java HotSpot(TM) 64-Bit Server VM (build 25.40-b25, mixed mode)
```

If you have verified the Java installation in your system, we can proceed with the ELK installation.

Installing Elasticsearch

When installing Elasticsearch during production, you can use the method described below, or the Debian or RPM packages provided on the download page.

 You can download the latest version of Elasticsearch from
`https://www.elastic.co/downloads/elasticsearch`.

```
curl -O https://download.elastic.co/elasticsearch/elasticsearch/
elasticsearch-1.5.2.tar.gz
```

 If you don't have cURL, you can use the following command to install it:
`sudo apt-get install curl`

Then, unpack the zip file on your local filesystem:

```
tar -zxvf elasticsearch-1.5.2.tar.gz
```

And then, go to the installation directory:

```
cd  elasticsearch-1.5.2
```

 Elastic, the company behind Elasticsearch, recently launched Elasticsearch 2.0 with some new aggregations, better compression options, simplified query DSL by merging query and filter concepts, and improved performance.
More details can be found in the official documentation:
`https://www.elastic.co/guide/en/elasticsearch/
reference/current/index.html`.

Running Elasticsearch

In order to run Elasticsearch, execute the following command:

```
$ bin/elasticsearch
```

Add the -d flag to run it in the background as a daemon process.

We can test it by running the following command in another terminal window:

```
curl 'http://localhost:9200/?pretty'
```

This shows you an output similar to this:

```
{
   "status" : 200,
   "name" : "Master",
   "cluster_name" : "elasticsearch",
   "version" : {
      "number" : "1.5.2",
      "build_hash" : "c88f77ffc81301dfa9dfd81ca2232f09588bd512",
      "build_timestamp" : "2015-05-13T13:05:36Z",
      "build_snapshot" : false,
      "lucene_version" : "4.10.3"
   },
   "tagline" : "You Know, for Search"
}
```

We can shut down Elasticsearch through the API as follows:

```
curl -XPOST 'http://localhost:9200/_shutdown'
```

Elasticsearch configuration

Elasticsearch configuration files are under the `config` folder in the Elasticsearch installation directory. The `config` folder has two files, namely `elasticsearch.yml` and `logging.yml`. The former will be used to specify configuration properties of different Elasticsearch modules, such as network address, paths, and so on, while the latter will specify logging-related configurations.

The configuration file is in the YAML format and the following sections are some of the parameters that can be configured.

Network Address

To specify the address where all network-based modules will bind and publish to:

```
network :
    host : 127.0.0.1
```

Paths

To specify paths for data and log files:

```
path:
   logs: /var/log/elasticsearch
   data: /var/data/elasticsearch
```

The cluster name

To give a name to a production cluster, which is used to discover and auto join nodes:

```
cluster:
  name: <NAME OF YOUR CLUSTER>
```

The node name

To change the default name of each node:

```
node:
  name: <NAME OF YOUR NODE>
```

Elasticsearch plugins

Elasticsearch has a variety of plugins that ease the task of managing indexes, cluster, and so on. Some of the mostly used ones are the Kopf plugin, Marvel, Sense, Shield, and so on, which will be covered in the subsequent chapters. Let's take a look at the Kopf plugin here.

Kopf is a simple web administration tool for Elasticsearch that is written in JavaScript, AngularJS, jQuery and Twitter bootstrap. It offers an easy way of performing common tasks on an Elasticsearch cluster. Not every single API is covered by this plugin, but it does offer a REST client, which allows you to explore the full potential of the Elasticsearch API.

In order to install the `elasticsearch-kopf` plugin, execute the following command from the Elasticsearch installation directory:

```
bin/plugin -install lmenezes/elasticsearch-kopf
```

Now, go to this address to see the interface: `http://localhost:9200/_plugin/kopf/`.

You can see a page similar to this, which shows Elasticsearch nodes, shards, a number of documents, size, and also enables querying the documents indexed.

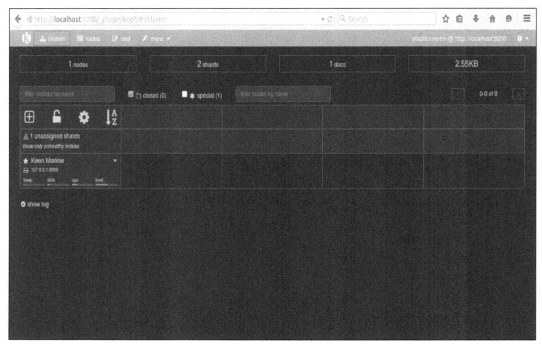

Elasticsearch Kopf UI

Installing Logstash

First, download the latest Logstash TAR file from the download page.

 Check for the latest Logstash release version at
https://www.elastic.co/downloads/logstash.

```
curl -O http://download.elastic.co/logstash/logstash/logstash-1.5.0.tar.
gz
```

Then, unpack the GZIP file on your local filesystem:

```
tar -zxvf logstash-1.5.0.tar.gz
```

Now, you can run Logstash with a basic configuration.

Running Logstash

Run Logstash using -e flag, followed by the configuration of standard input and output:

```
cd logstash-1.5.0
bin/logstash -e 'input { stdin { } } output { stdout {} }'
```

Now, when we type something in the command prompt, we will see its output in Logstash as follows:

```
hello logstash
2015-05-15T03:34:30.111Z 0.0.0.0 hello logstash
```

Here, we are running Logstash with the stdin input and the stdout output as this configuration prints whatever you type in a structured format as the output. The -e flag allows you to quickly test the configuration from the command line.

Now, let's try the codec setting for output for a pretty formatted output. Exit from the running Logstash by issuing a *Ctrl + C* command, and then we need to restart Logstash with the following command:

```
bin/logstash -e 'input { stdin { } } output { stdout { codec => rubydebug } }'
```

Now, enter some more test input:

```
Hello PacktPub

{
  "message" => " Hello PacktPub",
  "@timestamp" => "2015-05-20T23:48:05.335Z",
  "@version" => "1",
  "host" => "packtpub"
}
```

The output that you see is the most common output that we generally see from Logstash:

- "message" includes the complete input message or the event line
- "@timestamp" will include the timestamp of the time when the event was indexed; or if date filter is used, this value can also use one of the fields in the message to get a timestamp specific to the event
- "host" will generally represent the machine where this event was generated

Logstash with file input

Logstash can be easily configured to read from a log file as input.

For example, to read Apache logs from a file and output to a standard output console, the following configuration will be helpful:

```
input {
  file {
    type => "apache"
    path => "/user/packtpub/intro-to-elk/elk.log"
  }
}
output {
  stdout {
    codec => rubydebug
  }
}
```

Logstash with Elasticsearch output

Logstash can be configured to output all inputs to an Elasticsearch instance. This is the most common scenario in an ELK platform:

```
bin/logstash -e 'input { stdin { } } output { elasticsearch { host
= localhost } }'
```

Then type 'you know, for logs

You will be able to see indexes in Elasticsearch through
`http://localhost:9200/_search`.

Configuring Logstash

Logstash configuration files are in the JSON format. A Logstash config file has a separate section for each type of plugin that you want to add to the event processing pipeline. For example:

```
# This is a comment. You should use comments to describe
# parts of your configuration.
input {
  ...
}

filter {
  ...
```

```
}

output {
   . . .
}
```

Each section contains the configuration options for one or more plugins. If you specify multiple filters, they are applied in the order of their appearance in the configuration file.

When you run `logstash`, you use the `-flag` to read configurations from a configuration file or even from a folder containing multiple configuration files for each type of plugin—input, filter, and output:

bin/logstash -f ../conf/logstash.conf

> If you want to test your configurations for syntax errors before running them, you can simply check with the following command:
>
> `bin/logstash -configtest ../conf/logstash.conf`
>
> This command just checks the configuration without running `logstash`.

Logstash runs on JVM and consumes a hefty amount of resources to do so. Logstash, at times, has significant memory consumption. Obviously, this could be a great challenge when you want to send logs from a small machine without harming application performance.

In order to save resources, you can use the Logstash forwarder (previously known as Lumberjack). The forwarder uses Lumberjack's protocol, enabling you to securely ship compressed logs, thus reducing resource consumption and bandwidth. The sole input is file/s, while the output can be directed to multiple destinations.

Other options do exist as well, to send logs. You can use `rsyslog` on Linux machines, and there are other agents for Windows machines, such as `nxlog` and `syslog-ng`. There is another lightweight tool to ship logs called `Log-Courier` (`https://github.com/driskell/log-courier`), which is an enhanced fork of the Logstash forwarder with some improvements.

Installing Logstash forwarder

Download the latest Logstash forwarder release from the download page.

> Check for the latest Logstash forwarder release version at
> `https://www.elastic.co/downloads/logstash`.

Prepare a configuration file that contains input plugin details and ssl certificate details to establish a secure communication between your forwarder and indexer servers, and run it using the following command:

```
Logstash forwarder -config Logstash forwarder.conf
```

And in Logstash, we can use the Lumberjack plugin to get data from the forwarder:

```
input {
  lumberjack {
    # The port to listen on
    port => 12345

    # The paths to your ssl cert and key
    ssl_certificate => "path/to/ssl.crt"
    ssl_key => "path/to/ssl.key"

    # Set the type of log.
    type => "log type"
  }
```

Logstash plugins

Some of the most popular Logstash plugins are:

- Input plugin
- Filters plugin
- Output plugin

Input plugin

Some of the most popular Logstash input plugins are:

- **file**: This streams log events from a file
- **redis**: This streams events from a redis instance
- **stdin**: This streams events from standard input

- **syslog**: This streams syslog messages over the network
- **ganglia**: This streams ganglia packets over the network via udp
- **lumberjack**: This receives events using the lumberjack protocol
- **eventlog**: This receives events from Windows event log
- **s3**: This streams events from a file from an s3 bucket
- **elasticsearch**: This reads from the Elasticsearch cluster based on results of a search query

Filters plugin

Some of the most popular Logstash filter plugins are as follows:

- **date**: This is used to parse date fields from incoming events, and use that as Logstash timestamp fields, which can be later used for analytics
- **drop**: This drops everything from incoming events that matches the filter condition
- **grok**: This is the most powerful filter to parse unstructured data from logs or events to a structured format
- **multiline**: This helps parse multiple lines from a single source as one Logstash event
- **dns**: This filter will resolve an IP address from any fields specified
- **mutate**: This helps rename, remove, modify, and replace fields in events
- **geoip**: This adds geographic information based on IP addresses that are retrieved from `Maxmind` database

Output plugin

Some of the most popular Logstash output plugins are as follows:

- **file**: This writes events to a file on disk
- **e-mail**: This sends an e-mail based on some conditions whenever it receives an output
- **elasticsearch**: This stores output to the Elasticsearch cluster, the most common and recommended output for Logstash
- **stdout**: This writes events to standard output
- **redis**: This writes events to redis queue and is used as a broker for many ELK implementations
- **mongodb**: This writes output to mongodb
- **kafka**: This writes events to Kafka topic

Installing Kibana

Before we can install and run Kibana, it has certain prerequisites:

- Elasticsearch should be installed, and its HTTP service should be running on port `9200` (default).
- Kibana must be configured to use the host and port on which Elasticsearch is running (check out the following *Configuring Kibana* section).

Download the latest Kibana release from the download page.

> Check for the latest Kibana release version at
> `https://www.elastic.co/downloads/kibana`.

```
curl -O https://download.elastic.co/kibana/kibana/kibana-4.0.2-linux-x64.tar.gz
```

Then, unpack `kibana-4.0.2-linux-x64.tar.gz` on your local file system and create a soft link to use a short name.

```
tar -zxvf kibana-4.0.2-linux-x64.tar.gz
```

```
ln -s kibana-4.0.2-linux-x64 kibana
```

Then, you can explore the `kibana` folder:

```
cd kibana
```

Configuring Kibana

The Kibana configuration file is present in the `config` folder inside the `kibana` installation:

```
config/kibana.yml
```

Following are some of the important configurations for Kibana.

This controls which port to use.

```
port: 5601.
```

Property to set the host to bind the server is:

`host: "localhost".`

Set the `elasticsearch_url` to point at your Elasticsearch instance, which is `localhost` by default.

`elasticsearch_url: http://localhost:9200`

Running Kibana

Start Kibana manually by issuing the following command:

`bin/kibana`

You can verify the running Kibana instance on port `5601` by placing the following URL in the browser:

`http://localhost:5601`

This should fire up the Kibana UI for you.

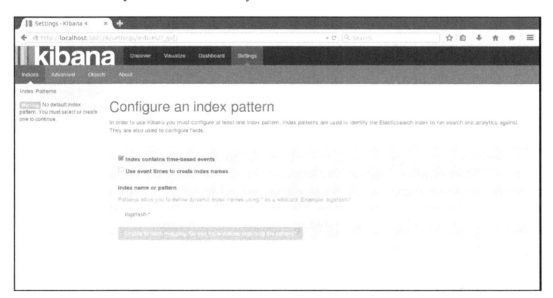

Kibana UI

We need to specify **Index name or pattern** that has to be used to show data indexed in Elasticsearch. By default, Kibana assumes the default index as `logstash-*` as it is assuming that data is being fed to Elasticsearch through Logstash. If you have changed the name of the index in Logstash output plugin configuration, then we need to change that accordingly.

Kibana 3 versus **Kibana 4**

Kibana 4 is a major upgrade over Kibana 3. Kibana 4 offers some advanced tools, which provides more flexibility in visualization and helps us use some of the advanced features of Elasticsearch. Kibana 3 had to be installed on a web server; Kibana 4 is released as a standalone application. Some of the new features in Kibana 4 as compared to Kibana 3 are as follows:

- Search results highlighting
- Shipping with its own web server and using Node.js on the backend
- Advanced aggregation-based analytics features, for example, unique counts, non-date histograms, ranges, and percentiles

Kibana interface

As you saw in the preceding screenshot of the Kibana UI, the Kibana interface consists of four main components — **Discover**, **Visualize**, **Dashboard**, and **Settings**.

Discover

The **Discover** page helps to interactively explore the data matching the selected index pattern. This page allows submitting search queries, filtering the search results, and viewing document data. Also, it gives us the count of matching results and statistics related to a field. If the **timestamp** field is configured in the indexed data, it will also display, by default, a histogram showing distribution of documents over time.

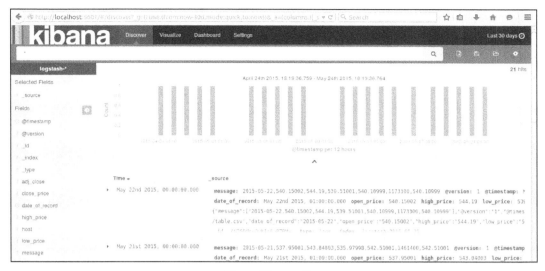

Kibana Discover Page

Visualize

The **Visualize** page is used to create new visualizations based on different data sources—a new interactive search, a saved search, or an existing saved visualization. Kibana 4 allows you to create the following visualizations in a new visualization wizard:

- Area chart
- Data table
- Line chart
- Markdown widget
- Metric
- Pie chart
- Tile map
- Vertical bar chart

These visualizations can be saved, used individually, or can be used in dashboards.

Kibana Visualize Page

Dashboard

Dashboard is a collection of saved visualizations in different groups. These visualizations can be arranged freely with a drag and drop kind of feature, and can be ordered as per the importance of the data. Dashboards can be easily saved, shared, and loaded at a later point in time.

Settings

The **Settings** page helps configure Elasticsearch indexes that we want to explore and configures various index patterns. Also, this page shows various indexed fields in one index pattern and data types of those fields. It also helps us create scripted fields, which are computed on the fly from the data.

Summary

In this chapter, we gathered a basic understanding of ELK stack, and also figured out why we need log analysis, and why ELK stack specifically. We also set up Elasticsearch, Logstash, and Kibana.

In the next chapter, we will look at how we can use our ELK stack installation to quickly build a data pipeline for analysis.

2
Building Your First Data Pipeline with ELK

In the previous chapter, we got familiar with each component of ELK Stack—Elasticsearch, Logstash, and Kibana. We got the components installed and configured. In this chapter, we will build our first basic data pipeline using ELK Stack. This will help us understand how easy it is to get together the components of ELK Stack to build an end-to-end analytics pipeline.

While running the example in this chapter, we assume that you already installed Elasticsearch, Logstash, and Kibana as described in *Chapter 1*, *Introduction to ELK Stack*.

Input dataset

For our example, the dataset that we are going to use here is the daily Google (GOOG) Quotes price dataset over a 6 month period from July 1, 2014 to December 31, 2014. This is a good dataset to understand how we can quickly analyze simple datasets, such as these, with ELK.

[This dataset can be easily downloaded from the following source:
`http://finance.yahoo.com/q/hp?s=GOOG`]

Data format for input dataset

The most significant fields of this dataset are `Date`, `Open Price`, `Close Price`, `High Price`, `Volume`, and `Adjusted Price`.

The following table shows some of the sample data from the dataset. The actual dataset is in the CSV format.

Date	Open	High	Low	Close	Volume	Adj Close
Dec 31, 2014	531.25	532.60	525.80	526.40	1,368,200	526.40
Dec 30, 2014	528.09	531.15	527.13	530.42	876,300	530.42
Dec 29, 2014	532.19	535.48	530.01	530.33	2,278,500	530.33
Dec 26, 2014	528.77	534.25	527.31	534.03	1,036,000	534.03
Dec 24, 2014	530.51	531.76	527.02	528.77	705,900	528.77
Dec 23, 2014	527.00	534.56	526.29	530.59	2,197,600	530.59
Dec 22, 2014	516.08	526.46	516.08	524.87	2,723,800	524.87
Dec 19, 2014	511.51	517.72	506.91	516.35	3,690,200	516.35
Dec 18, 2014	512.95	513.87	504.70	511.10	2,926,700	511.10
Dec 17, 2014	497.00	507.00	496.81	504.89	2,883,200	504.89
Dec 16, 2014	511.56	513.05	489.00	495.39	3,964,300	495.39
Dec 15, 2014	522.74	523.10	513.27	513.80	2,813,400	513.80
Dec 12, 2014	523.51	528.50	518.66	518.66	1,994,600	518.66
Dec 11, 2014	527.80	533.92	527.10	528.34	1,610,800	528.34
Dec 10, 2014	533.08	536.33	525.56	526.06	1,712,300	526.06

We need to put this data into a location from where ELK Stack can access it for further analysis.

We will look at some of the top entries of the CSV file using the Unix `head` command as follows:

```
$ head GOOG.csv
2014-12-31,531.25244,532.60236,525.80237,526.4024,1368200,526.4024
2014-12-30,528.09241,531.1524,527.13239,530.42242,876300,530.42242
2014-12-29,532.19244,535.48242,530.01337,530.3324,2278500,530.3324
2014-12-26,528.7724,534.25244,527.31238,534.03247,1036000,534.03247
2014-12-24,530.51245,531.76141,527.0224,528.7724,705900,528.7724
2014-12-23,527.00238,534.56244,526.29236,530.59241,2197600,530.59241
2014-12-22,516.08234,526.4624,516.08234,524.87238,2723800,524.87238
2014-12-19,511.51233,517.72235,506.9133,516.35229,3690200,516.35229
2014-12-18,512.95233,513.87231,504.7023,511.10233,2926700,511.10233
```

Each row represents the Quote price data for a particular date separated by a comma.

Now, when we are familiar with the data, we will set up the ELK Stack where we can parse and process the data using Logstash, index it in Elasticsearch, and then build beautiful visualizations in Kibana.

Configuring Logstash input

As we already know, Logstash has a rich set of plugins for different types of inputs, outputs and filters, which can read, parse, and filter data as per our needs. We will utilize the `file` input plugin to read the source file.

A `file` input plugin streams events from the input file, and each event is assumed as a single line. It automatically detects file rotation and handles it. It maintains the location where it left reading, and will automatically detect the new data if configured correctly. It reads files in a similar manner:

```
tail -0f
```

In general, a `file` input plugin configuration will look as follows:

```
input {

file {
    path => #String (path of the files) (required)
    start_position => #String (optional, default "end")
    tags => #array (optional)
    type => #string (optional)
}

}
```

- `path`: The `path` field is the only required field in `file` input plugin, which represents the path of the file from where input events have to be processed.

- `start_position`: This defines from where Logstash starts reading input files. Values can be `"beginning"` or `"end"`. The default value is `"end"` which caters to the needs of reading live streams. If we need to read some historic data, it can be set to `"beginning"`.

- `tags`: `tags` represents any number of strings as an array that can be utilized later to filter and process events based on tags assigned to them.

- `type`: The `type` field can be used to mark a specific type of events, which helps to filter and search them later. Type is added to the document that is stored in Elasticsearch, and can later be viewed in Kibana under the `_type` field. For example, we can assign type as `"error_logs"` or `"info_logs"`.

Let's configure Logstash for our input dataset:

```
input{
file{
path =>"/opt/logstash/input/GOOG.csv"
```

```
start_position =>"beginning"
  }
}
```

We will provide the path of the CSV file in the `path` attribute, and as our dataset is historic, we will use `start_position` as `"beginning"`.

Filtering and processing input

Once we configure the input file, we need to filter the input based on our needs so that we can identify which fields we need, and process them as per the required analysis.

A `filter` plugin will perform the intermediary processing on the input event. We can apply the filter conditionally based on certain fields.

Since our input file is a CSV file, we will use the `csv` filter for the same. The `csv` filter takes an event field that contains CSV formatted data, parses it, and stores it as individual fields. It can also parse data with any separator other than commas. A typical `csv` filter is as follows:

```
filter {
    csv {
        columns => #Array of column names.
        separator => #String ; default -","
    }
}
```

The `attribute` columns take the name of fields in our CSV file, which is optional. By default, the columns will be named as `column 1`, `column 2`, and so on.

The `attribute` separator defines what character is used to separate the different columns in the file. The default is a comma, but it can be any other separator too.

In our example, we can specify a simple `csv` filter as follows:

```
filter {
    csv {
    columns =>
["date_of_record","open","high","low","close","volume","adj_close"
]
        separator => ","
    }
}
```

Here, we specified the column names as defined in our CSV file, and explicitly defined the separator as a comma just to make it clear.

Now, we are done with `csv` filter configuration, but we still need to do some intermediary processing on the columns to associate specific data types with our columns.

First of all, we need to specify which column represents the `date` field so that it can be explicitly indexed as date type and can be used to filter based on date. Logstash has a specific filter called `date` for the same. A typical `date` filter looks as follows:

```
filter {
  date {
    match =>  # array (optional), default: []
    target =>  # string (optional), default: "@timestamp"
    timezone => # string (optional)
  }

}
```

Here, in the `match` attribute, we define an array, which is in the `[field, formats]` format; that is, field, followed by a set of time formats that can be applied to that field. For example, if our log file has multiple formats, we can use the the following code:

```
match => [ "date_field", "MMM dd YYY HH:mm:ss",
           "MMM  d YYY HH:mm:ss",  "MMddYYYY","ISO8601" ]
```

> **Date formats in Logstash**: Date formats allowed are as per the allowed JodaTime `DateTimeFormat` library:
> `http://joda-time.sourceforge.net/apidocs/org/joda/time/format/DateTimeFormat.html`

As per our `date` format, our `date` filter will be as follows:

```
date{
match => ["date_of_record", "yyyy-MM-dd"]
target => "@timestamp"
}
```

The `target` filter defines where to map the matching timestamp. By default, it maps to `@timestamp` (the field that represents the time stamp of the event, which defaults to the time when the event was captured). In our case, since we are taking some historic data, we don't want the event captured time to be in `@timestamp`, but the date of record. We will map our `date` field to `@timestamp`. It is not mandatory to define this, but recommended to use.

After updating the data type of date fields, the next operation we require is updating the data type of fields, which we need for numeric comparisons or operations. By default, the value will be of string data type. We will convert them to integers so that we can perform some aggregations and comparisons on the data.

We will use mutate filter for the conversion of fields to a specific data type. This filter helps perform general mutations on the fields, which includes modifications of data types, renaming, replacing fields, and removing fields. It can also help merge two fields, perform uppercase and lowercase conversions, split and strip fields, and so on.

A typical mutate filter looks like this:

```
filter {
  mutate {

    convert => # hash of field and data type (optional)
    join =>  # hash of fields to be joined (optional)
    lowercase =>  # array of fields to be converted (optional)
    merge =>  # hash  of fields to be merged (optional)
    rename =>  # hash of original and rename field (optional)
    replace => # hash of fields to replaced with (optional)
    split =>  # hash of fields to be split (optional)
    strip => # array of fields (optional)
    uppercase =>  # array of fields (optional)
  }

}
```

Let's see what our mutate filter looks like:

```
mutate {

convert => ["open","float"]

convert => ["high ","float"]

convert => ["low ","float"]
convert => ["close ","float"]

convert => ["volume","integer"]
convert => ["adj_close","float"]

}
```

We are using the convert functionality to convert our price and volume fields to integer. Valid data types are "integer", "float", and "string".

Putting data to Elasticsearch

Now that we have set up the data to be consumed by a CSV file into Logstash, followed by parsing and processing based on the data type needed, we now need to put the data in Elasticsearch so that we can index the different fields and consume them later via the Kibana interface.

We will use the `output` plugin of Logstash for an `elasticsearch` output.

A typical `elasticsearch` plugin configuration looks like this:

```
output {

  elasticsearch {

    action =>  # string (optional), default: "index"

    cluster =>  # string (optional)

    host =>  # string (optional)

    document_id =>  # string (optional), default: nil


    index =>  # string (optional), default: "logstash-%{+YYYY.MM.dd}"
    index_type =>  # string (optional)
    port =>  # string (optional)
    protocol =>  # string, one of ["node", "transport", "http"]
(optional)
  }
}
```

- `action`: This specifies what action to perform on incoming documents. The default is `"index"` and possible values are `"index"` or `"delete"`. The `"index"` value will index a document and `"delete"` will delete a document based on document ID.

- `cluster`: This is the name of the cluster set in `elasticsearch`.

- `host`: This is the hostname or IP address of the `elasticsearch`.

- `document_id`: This is the document ID of the index; it is useful to delete or overwrite the existing entries.

- `index`: This is the index name to which the incoming events have to be written. By default, it is indexed based on each day, and named as `"logstash-%{+YYYY.MM.dd}"`.

- index_type: This specifies the index type to write events to. This is to ensure that you write similar types of events to the same index type.
- port: This specifies the port to be used for the elasticsearch service.
- protocol: This specifies the protocol to be used to connect with Elasticsearch. The values are "http", "node", and "transport".

Now, let's take a look at our elasticsearch output configuration:

```
output{

elasticsearch {

host => "localhost"

}
}
```

We used the default value for index and most of the other settings.

Now, when we have seen how individual plugins are configured, let's take a look at what the overall Logstash configuration looks like:

```
input{
file{

path =>"/opt/logstash/input/GOOG.csv"
start_position =>"beginning"

}

}

filter{
csv{

columns =>
["date_of_record","open","high","low","close","volume","adj_close"]

separator => ","
}

date {

match => ["date_of_record","yyyy-MM-dd"]
```

```
}

mutate {

convert => ["open","float"]

convert => ["high","float"]

convert => ["low","float"]

convert => ["close","float"]

convert => ["volume","integer"]

convert => ["adj_close","float"]
}

}
output{

elasticsearch {

host => "localhost"

}

}
```

We will save this configuration in the Logstash installation folder with the name logstash.conf, and as we saw earlier, we can run Logstash with this configuration using the following command:

 Before running Logstash with this configuration, make sure the Elasticsearch is running as per the instructions in the previous chapter.

```
$ bin/logstash -f logstash.conf
```

Logstash will start to run with the defined configuration and keep on indexing all incoming events to the elasticsearch indexes. You may see an output similar to this on the console:

```
May 31, 2015 4:04:54 PM org.elasticsearch.node.internal.InternalNode
start
INFO: [logstash-4004-9716] started
Logstash startup completed
```

At this point, we can open the `elasticsearch Kopf` plugin console to verify whether we have some documents indexed already, and we can also query the documents.

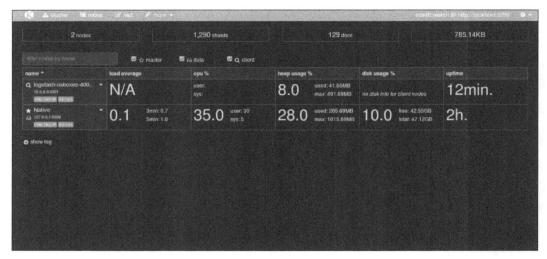

Elasticsearch Kopf interface

As we can see that there are 129 documents indexed already, we verified that our Logstash configuration worked well.

Visualizing with Kibana

Now when you verify that your data is indexed successfully in Elasticsearch, we can go ahead and look at the Kibana interface to get some useful analytics from the data.

Running Kibana

As described in the previous chapter, we will start the Kibana service from the Kibana installation directory.

```
$ bin/kibana
```

Now, let's see Kibana up and running similar to the following screenshot on the browser, by going to the following URL:

```
http://localhost:5601
```

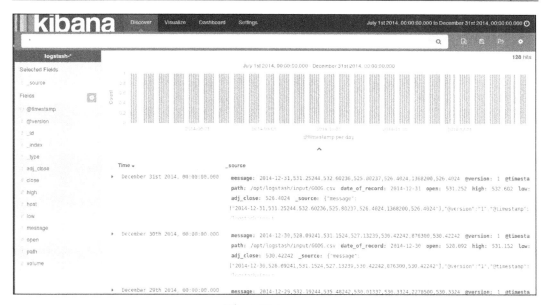

Kibana Discover page

As we already set up Kibana to take **logstash-*** indexes by default, it displays the indexed data as a histogram of counts, and the associated data as fields in the JSON format.

First of all, we need to set the `date` filter to filter based on our date range so that we can build our analysis on the same. Since we took data from July 1, 2014 to December 31, 2014, we will configure our `date` filter for the same.

Clicking on the **Time Filter** icon at the extreme top-right corner, we can set an Absolute **Time Filter** based on our range as follows:

Kibana Time Filter

Now, we are all set to build beautiful visualizations on the collected dataset using the rich set of visualization features that Kibana provides.

Before we build the visualization, let's confirm whether all fields are indexed properly with their associated data types so that we can perform the appropriate operations on them.

For this, let's click on the **Settings** page at the top of the screen and select the **logstash-*** index pattern on the left of the screen. The page looks something like this:

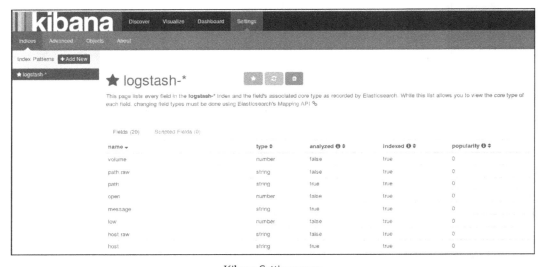

Kibana Settings page

It shows all our fields that were indexed, their data types, index status, and popularity value.

Kibana visualizations

Let's build some basic visualizations from the Kibana visualizations page, and we will use them later in dashboard.

Click on the visualization page link at the top of the Kibana home page, and click on the new visualization icon.

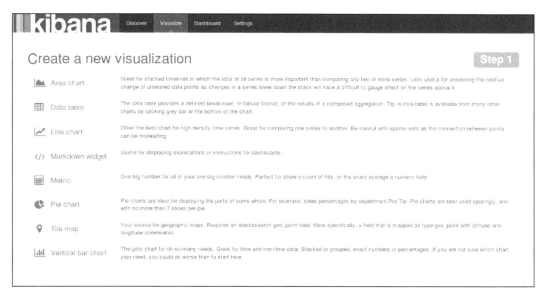

Kibana visualization menu

Building a line chart

The first visualization that we will build is a line chart showing weekly close price index movement for the GOOG script over a six month period.

Select **Line Chart** from the visualization menu, and then we'll select **Y-Axis** metrics as **Max**, and **Field** as **close**. In the **buckets** section, select **Aggregation** as **Date Histogram** based on the **@timestamp** field, and **Interval** as **Weekly**, and click on **Apply**.

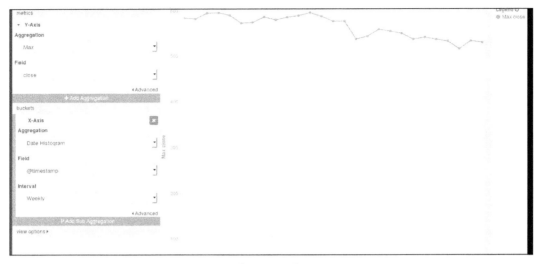

Kibana Line chart

Now, save the visualization using some name for the line chart, which we will pull into the dashboard later.

Building a bar chart

We will build a vertical bar chart representing the movement of weekly traded volumes over a six month period.

Select **Vertical Bar Chart** from the visualization menu, and select **Y-Axis Aggregation** as **Sum**, and **Field** as **volume**. In the **buckets** section, select **X-Axis Aggregation** as **Date Histogram**, and **Field** as **@timestamp**, and **Interval** as **Weekly**. Click on **Apply** to see a vertical bar chart representing the weekly total volume traded over a six month period.

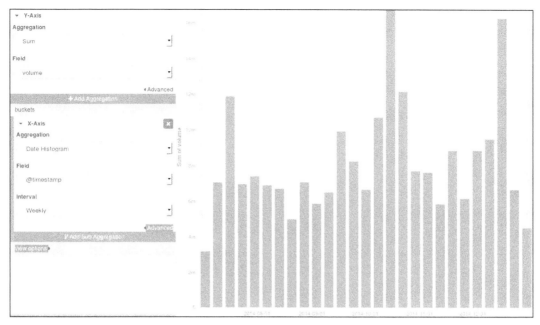

Kibana Vertical Bar Chart

Now, save the visualization using some name for the bar chart, which we will pull into the dashboard later.

Building a Metric

Metric represents one big number that we want to show as something special about data.

We will show the **Highest Volume Traded** in a single day in a six month period using Metric.

Click on **Metric** in the visualization menu, and select **Metric Aggregation** as **Max**, **Field** as **volume**. Click on **Apply** to see the result of visualization on the right as follows:

Kibana Metric

Now, save the visualization using some name for the **Metric**, which we will pull into the dashboard later.

Building a data table

Data tables are meant to show detailed breakdowns in a tabular format for results of some composed aggregations.

We will create a data table of **Monthly Average** volume traded over six months.

Click on **Metric** in the visualization menu, and select **Metric Aggregation** as **Max**, **Field** as **volume**. Click on **Apply** to see the result of visualization on the right as follows:

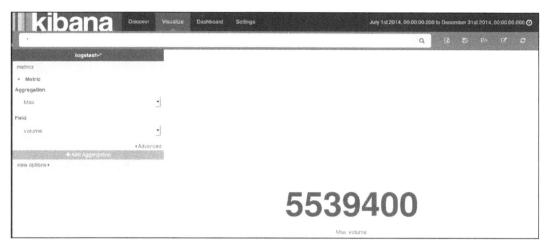

Kibana Metric

Now, save the visualization using some name for the **Metric**, which we will pull into the dashboard later.

Building a data table

Data tables are meant to show detailed breakdowns in a tabular format for results of some composed aggregations.

We will create a data table of **Monthly Average** volume traded over six months.

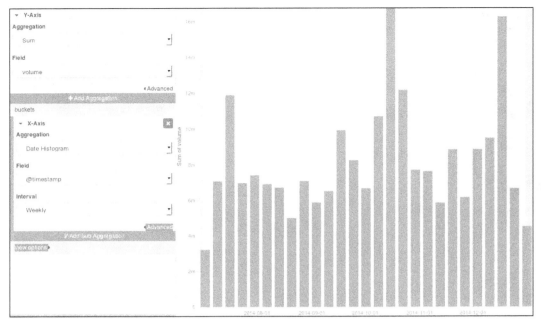

Kibana Vertical Bar Chart

Now, save the visualization using some name for the bar chart, which we will pull into the dashboard later.

Building a Metric

Metric represents one big number that we want to show as something special about data.

We will show the **Highest Volume Traded** in a single day in a six month period using Metric.

Select **Data table** from the visualization menu, click on **split rows** and select **Aggregation** as **Average** and **Fields** as **volume**. In the **buckets** section, select **Aggregation** as **Date Histogram**, **Fields** as **@timestamp**, and **Interval** as **Monthly**. Click on **Apply** to see the image as in the following screenshot:

Kibana Data table

Now, save the visualization using some name for the data table, which we will pull into the dashboard later.

After we have built some visualizations, let's build a dashboard that includes these visualizations.

Select the dashboard page link at top of the page, and click on the **Add Visualization** link to select visualizations from your saved visualizations and arrange them.

The Dashboard, after including a line chart, bar chart, data table, and Metric, looks like this:

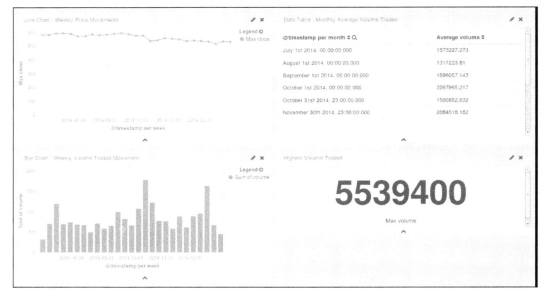

Kibana Dashboard

Now, we can save this dashboard using the save button, and it can be pulled later and shared easily.

Dashboards can be embedded as an IFrame in other systems or can be directly shared as links.

Click on the **share** button to see the options to share:

Kibana Share options

If you have completed everything up to this point, then you have successfully set up your first ELK data pipeline.

Summary

In this chapter, we saw how you can utilize different input, filter, and output plugins in Logstash to gather, parse, and index data to Elasticsearch, and later utilize the Kibana interface to query and visualize over Elasticsearch indexes. We also built some visualizations, and a dashboard using those visualizations. We successfully built our first data pipeline using ELK Stack. In the coming chapters, we will look at individual components in more detail.

3
Collect, Parse and Transform Data with Logstash

By now, we should have a basic understanding of ELK Stack and what role it plays in log analysis or event analysis systems. In *Chapter 2*, *Building Your First Data Pipeline with ELK*, we built analytics over the GOOG stock price data with the ELK Stack configuration, and also understood role of each component of the stack in the pipeline.

In this chapter, we will get into more detail on Logstash, the most important component of the ELK Stack, and see how Logstash helps collect, parse, and transform any format and any type of data to a common format, which can be used to build a wide variety of analytics systems across many applications.

We saw in *Chapter 1*, *Introduction to ELK Stack*, the importance of log analysis and problem with log analysis methods. Also, there are a variety of log formats, and date and time formats in logs. Often these logs are customized to each application and require expert knowledge to gather essential information out of them. Now, we will see how Logstash provides us with a variety of plugins that help us overcome all of these problems and build easily-configurable and manageable visualizations on top of it.

In this chapter, while explaining various configurations of Logstash plugins, we assume that you have installed Logstash, as explained in *Chapter 1*, *Introduction to ELK Stack*, and have the basic configuration set up and running. If you do not, you should get Logstash installed and run a basic `stdin`, `stdout` configuration and then resume this chapter so that you can try out some configuration options based on the explanations.

Configuring Logstash

As we have seen in previous chapters, a general Logstash plugin configuration looks like this:

```
input {

}

filter {

}

output {

}
```

A Logstash configuration consists of a series of `input`, `filter`, and `output` plugins and their corresponding properties. Each plugin plays an important role towards parsing, processing, and finally putting the data in the required format. Input plugins generate the event, filters modify them, and output will ship them to other systems.

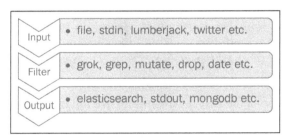

Logstash plugins

Logstash plugins

Logstash has a variety of plugins to help integrate it with a variety of input and output sources. Let's explore the various plugins available.

Listing all plugins in Logstash

You can execute the following command to list all available plugins in your installed Logstash version:

```
bin/plugin list
```

Also, you can list all plugins containing a name fragment by executing this command:

```
bin/plugin list <namefragment>
```

To list all plugins for group names, input, output, or filter, we can execute this command:

```
bin/plugin list --group <group name>
bin/plugin list --group output
```

Before exploring various plugin configurations, let's take a look at the data types and conditional expressions used in various Logstash configurations.

Data types for plugin properties

A Logstash plugin requires certain settings or properties to be set. Those properties have certain values that belong to one of the following important data types.

Array

An array is collection of values for a property.

An example can be seen as follows:

```
path => ["value1","value2"]
```

 The => sign is the assignment operator that is used for all properties of configuration values in Logstash configuration.

Boolean

A boolean value is either `true` or `false` (without quotes).

An example can be seen as follows:

```
periodic_flush => false
```

Codec

Codec is actually not a data type but a way to encode or decode data at input or output.

An example can be seen as follows:

```
codec => "json"
```

This instance specifies that this codec, at output, will encode all output in JSON format.

Hash

Hash is basically a key value pair collection. It is specified as `"key" => "value"` and multiple values in a collection are separated by a space.

An example can be seen as follows:

```
match => {
"key1" => "value1" "key2" => "value2"}
```

String

String represents a sequence of characters enclosed in quotes.

An example can be seen as follows:

```
value => "Welcome to ELK"
```

Comments

Comments begin with the # character.

An example can be seen as follows:

```
#this represents a comment
```

Field references

Fields can be referred to using [field_name] or nested fields using [level1][level2].

Logstash conditionals

Logstash conditionals are used to filter events or log lines under certain conditions. Conditionals in Logstash are handled like other programming languages and work with if, if else and else statements. Multiple if else blocks can be nested.

Syntax for conditionals is as follows:

```
if  <conditional expression1>{
#some statements here.
}
else if  <conditional expression2>{
#some statements here.
}
else{
#some statements here.
}
```

Conditionals work with comparison operators, boolean operators and unary operators:

Comparison operators include:

- **Equality operators**: ==, !=, <, >, <=, >=
- **Regular expressions**: =~, !~
- **Inclusion**: in, not in
- Boolean operators include and, or, nand, xor
- Unary operators include !

Let's take a look at this with an example:

```
filter {
  if [action] == "login" {
    mutate { remove => "password" }
  }
}
```

Multiple expressions can be specified in a single statement using boolean operators.

An example can be seen as follows:

```
output {
  # Send Email on Production Errors
  if [loglevel] == "ERROR" and [deployment] == "production" {
   email{


   }

  }
}
```

Types of Logstash plugins

The following are types of Logstash plugins:

- Input
- Filter
- Output
- Codec

Now let's take a look at some of the most important input, output, filter and codec plugins, which will be useful for building most of the log analysis pipeline use cases.

Input plugins

An input plugin is used to configure a set of events to be fed to Logstash. Some of the most important input plugins are:

file

The `file` plugin is used to stream events and log lines files to Logstash. It automatically detects file rotations, and reads from the point last read by it.

> The Logstash `file` plugin maintains `sincedb` files to track the current positions in files being monitored. By default it writes `sincedb` files at $HOME/`.sincedb*` path. The location and frequency can be altered using `sincedb_path` and `sincedb_write_interval` properties of the plugin.

A most basic file configuration looks like this:

```
input{
file{
path => "/path/to/logfiles"
}
```

The only required configuration property is the *path* to the files. Let's look at how we can make use of some of the configuration properties of the file plugin to read different types of files.

Configuration options

The following configuration options are available for the file input plugin:

add_field

It is used to add a field to incoming events, its value type is `Hash`, and default value is `{}`.

Let's take the following instance as an example:

```
add_field => { "input_time" => "%{@timestamp}" }
```

codec

It is used to specify a codec, which can decode a specific type of input.

For example: `codec => "json"` is used to decode the `json` type of input.

The default value of codec is `"plain"`.

delimiter

It is used to specify a delimiter, which identifies separate lines. By default, it is `"\n"`.

exclude

To exclude certain types of files from the input path, the data type is `array`.

Let's take the following instance as an example:

```
path =>["/app/packtpub/logs/*"]
exclude => "*.gz"
```

This will exclude all gzip files from input.

path

This is the only required configuration for the file plugin. It specifies an array of path locations from where to read logs and events.

sincedb_path

It specifies the location where to write the `sincedb` files, which keeps track of the current position of files being monitored. The default is `$HOME/.sincedb*`

sincedb_write_interval

It specifies how often (number in seconds), the `sincedb` files that keep track of the current position of monitored files, are to be written. The default is 15 seconds.

start_position

It has two values: `"beginning"` and `"end"`. It specifies where to start reading incoming files from. The default value is `"end"`, as in most situations this is used for live streaming data. Although, if you are working on old data, it can be set to `"beginning"`.

 This option has impact only when a file is being read for the first time, called `"first contact"`, as it maintains the location in the `"sincedb"` location. So for the next setting, this option has no impact unless you decide to remove the `sincedb` files.

tags

It specifies the array of tags that can be added to incoming events. Adding tags to your incoming events helps with processing later, when using conditionals. It is often helpful to tag certain data as `"processed"` and use those tags to decide a future course of action.

For example, if we specify `"processed"` in tags:

```
tags =>["processed"]
```

In filter, we can check in conditionals:

```
filter{
if  "processed" in tags[]{

}
}
```

type

The type option is really helpful to process the different type of incoming streams using Logstash. You can configure multiple input paths for different type of events, just give a type name, and then you can filter them separately and process.

Let's take the following instance as an example:

```
input {
file{
path => ["var/log/syslog/*"]
type => "syslog"
}
file{
path => ["var/log/apache/*"]
type => "apache"
}
}
```

In filter, we can filter based on type:

```
filter {
if [type] == "syslog" {
grok {

}

}
if [type] == "apache" {
grok {

}
}
}
```

As in the preceding example, we have configured a separate type for incoming files; "syslog" and "apache". Later in filtering the stream, we can specify conditionals to filter based on this type.

stdin

The stdin plugin is used to stream events and log lines from standard input.

A basic configuration for stdin looks like this:

```
stdin {

}
```

When we configure stdin like this, whatever we type in the console will go as input to the Logstash event pipeline. This is mostly used as the first level of testing of configuration before plugging in the actual file or event input.

Configuration options

The following configuration options are available for the stdin input plugin:

add_field

The add_field configuration for stdin is the same as add_field in the file input plugin and is used for similar purposes.

codec

It is used to decode incoming data before passing it on to the data pipeline. The default value is "line".

tags

The tags configuration for stdin is the same as tags in the file input plugin and is used for similar purposes.

type

The type configuration for stdin is the same as type in the file input plugin and is used for similar purposes.

twitter

You may need to analyze a Twitter stream based on a topic of interest for various purposes, such as sentiment analysis, trending topics analysis, and so on. The twitter plugin is helpful to read events from the Twitter streaming API. This requires a consumer key, consumer secret, keyword, oauth token, and oauth token secret to work.

These details can be obtained by registering an application on the Twitter developer API page (https://dev.twitter.com/apps/new):

```
twitter {
    consumer_key => "your consumer key here"
    keywords => "keywords which you want to filter on streams"
    consumer_secret => "your consumer secret here"
    oauth_token => "your oauth token here"
    oauth_token_secret => "your oauth token secret here"
}
```

Configuration options

The following configuration options are available for the twitter input plugin:

add_field

The add_field configuration for the twitter plugin is the same as add_field in the file input plugin and is used for similar purposes.

codec

The codec configuration for twitter is the same as the codec plugin in the file input plugin and is used for similar purposes.

consumer_key

This is a required configuration with no default value. Its value can be obtained from the Twitter app registration page. Its value is the String type.

consumer_secret

The same as consumer_key, its value can be obtained from the Twitter dev app registration.

full_tweet

This is a boolean configuration with the default value; false. It specifies whether to record a full tweet object obtained from the Twitter streaming API.

keywords

This is an array type required configuration, with no default value. It specifies a set of keywords to track from the Twitter stream.

An example can be seen as follows:

```
keywords  => ["elk","packtpub"]
```

oauth_token

The oauth_token option is also obtained from the Twitter dev API page.

 After you get your consumer key and consumer secret, click on **Create My Access Token** to create your oauth token and oauth token secret.

oauth_token_secret

The oauth_token_secret option is obtained from the Twitter dev API page.

tags

The `tags` configuration for the `twitter` input plugin is the same as `tags` in the `file` input plugin and is used for similar purposes.

type

`type` configuration for `twitter` input plugins is the same as `type` in the `file` input plugin and is used for similar purposes.

lumberjack

The `lumberjack` plugin is useful to receive events via the `lumberjack` protocol that is used in Logstash forwarder.

The basic required configuration option for the `lumberjack` plugin looks like this:

```
lumberjack {
    port =>
    ssl_certificate =>
    ssl_key =>
}
```

> Lumberjack or Logstash forwarder is a light weight log shipper used to ship log events from source systems. Logstash is quite a memory consuming process, so installing it on every node from where you want to ship data is not recommended. Logstash forwarder is a light weight version of Logstash, which provides low latency, secure and reliable transfer, and provides low resource usage.
>
> More details about Lumberjack or Logstash forwarder can be found from here:
>
> https://github.com/elastic/logstash-forwarder

Configuration options

The following configuration options are available for the `lumberjack` input plugin:

add_field

The `add_field` configuration for the `lumberjack` plugin is the same as `add_field` in the `file` input plugin and is used for similar purposes.

codec

The `codec` configuration for the `lumberjack` plugin is the same as the `codec` plugin in the `file` input plugin and is used for similar purposes.

host

It specifies the host on which to listen to. The default value: `"0.0.0.0"`.

port

This is a number type required configuration and it specifies the port to listen to. There is no default value.

ssl_certificate

It specifies the path to the SSL certificate to be used for the connection. It is a required setting.

An example is as follows:

```
ssl_certificate => "/etc/ssl/logstash.pub"
```

ssl_key

It specifies the path to the SSL key that has to be used for the connection. It is also a required setting.

An example is as follows:

```
ssl_key => "/etc/ssl/logstash.key"
```

ssl_key_passphrase

It specifies the SSL key passphrase that has to be used for the connection.

tags

The `tags` configuration for the `lumberjack` input plugin is the same as `tags` in the `file` input plugin and is used for similar purposes.

type

The `type` configuration for the `lumberjack` input plugins is the same as `type` in the `file` input plugin and is used for similar purposes.

redis

The `redis` plugin is used to read events and logs from the `redis` instance.

 Redis is often used in ELK Stack as a broker for incoming log data from the Logstash forwarder, which helps to queue data until the time the indexer is ready to ingest logs. This helps to keep the system in check under heavy load.

The basic configuration of the `redis` input plugin looks like this:

```
redis {
}
```

Configuration options

The following configuration options are available for the `redis` input plugin:

add_field

The `add_field` configuration for `redis` is the same as `add_field` in the `file` input plugin and is used for similar purposes.

codec

The `codec` configuration for `redis` is the same as `codec` in the `file` input plugin and is used for similar purposes.

data_type

The `data_type` option can have a value as either `"list"`, `"channel"` or `"pattern_channel"`.

From the Logstash documentation for the `redis` plugin (https://www.elastic.co/guide/en/logstash/current/plugins-inputs-redis.html):

> *"If* `redis_type` *is* `list`, *then we will BLPOP the key. If* `redis_type` *is* `channel`, *then we will SUBSCRIBE to the key. If* `redis_type` *is* `pattern_channel`, *then we will PSUBSCRIBE to the key."*

 While using `redis` on the consumer and publisher side, key and `data_type` should be the same on both sides.

host

It specifies the hostname of the `redis` server. The default value is `"127.0.0.1"`.

key

It specifies the key for redis; `"list"` or `"channel"`.

password

It is a `password` type configuration that specifies the password to be used for connection.

port

It specifies the port on which the `redis` instance is running. The default is `6379`.

An extensive list and latest documentation on all available Logstash input plugins is available at `https://www.elastic.co/guide/en/logstash/current/input-plugins.html`.

Now that we have seen some of the most important input plugins for Logstash, let's have a look at some output plugins.

Output plugins

Logstash provides a wide variety of output plugins that help integrate incoming events with almost any type of destination. Let's look at some of the most used output plugins in detail.

csv

The `csv` plugin is used to write a CSV file as output, specifying the fields in `csv` and the path of the file.

The basic configuration of the `csv` output plugin looks like this:

```
csv {
    fields => ["date","open_price","close_price"]
    path => "/path/to/file.csv"
}
```

Configuration options

The following are the configuration options available for the `csv` plugin:

codec

It is used to encode the data before it goes out of Logstash. The default value is `"plain"`, which will output data as it is.

csv_options

The `csv_options` option is used to specify advanced options for the `csv` output. It includes changing the default column and row separator.

An example is as follows:

```
csv_options => {"col_sep" => "\t" "row_sep" => "\r\n"}
```

fields

The `fields` setting is a required setting that is used to specify the fields for the output CSV file. It is specified as an array of field names and written in the same order as in the array. There is no default value for this setting.

gzip

The `gzip` setting is a boolean type of setting that specifies whether to output as a gzip compressed format or not. The default is `false`.

path

The `path` setting is a required setting and is used to specify the path to the CSV file.

file

The `file` output plugin, just like the `file` input plugin, will be used to write events to a file in the file system.

The basic configuration of the `file` output plugin looks like this:

```
file
{
path = > "path/to/file"
}
```

Configuration options

The available configuration options are:

- `codec`
- `gzip`
- `max_size`
- `path`

Most of these configuration options have been covered earlier and are well understood by their name.

email

The `email` plugin is a very important output plugin as it is very useful to send e-mails for certain events and failure scenarios.

The basic required configuration looks like this:

```
email {
    to => "abc@example.com"
}
```

Configuration options

The following configuration options are available for the `email` plugin:

attachments

The `attachments` option is an array of file paths to be attached with the e-mail. The default value is `[]`

body

The `body` option specifies the body of the e-mail in plain text format. The default value is `""`.

cc

The `cc` option specifies the list of e-mails to be included as the cc addresses in the e-mail. It accepts multiple e-mail IDs in a comma separated format.

from

The `from` option specifies the e-mail address to be used as the sender address in the e-mail. The default value is `"logstash.alert@nowhere.com"` and must be overridden as per the type of alerts or system.

to

The `to` option is a required setting that specifies the receiver address for the e-mail. It can also be expressed as a string of comma separated e-mail addresses.

htmlbody

The `htmlbody` option specifies the body of the e-mail in HTML format. It includes HTML mark-up tags in the e-mail body.

replyto

The `replyto` option specifies the e-mail address to be used for the `Reply-To` field for the e-mail.

subject

The `subject` option specifies the subject for the e-mail. The default value is `""`.

elasticsearch

The `elasticsearch` plugin is the most important plugin used in ELK Stack, because it is where you will want to write your output to be stored to analyze later in Kibana.

We will take a look at ElasticSearch in more detail in *Chapter 5, Why Do We Need Elasticsearch in ELK?*, but let's look at the configuration options for this plugin here:

The basic configuration for the `elasticsearch` plugin looks like this:

```
elasticsearch {
}
```

Configuration options

Some of the most important configuration options are mentioned as follows:

option	data type	required	default value
action	string	N	"index"
bind_host	string	N	
bind_port	number	N	
cacert	a valid system path	N	
cluster	string	N	
document_id	string	N	
document_type	string	N	
host	array	N	
index	string	N	"logstash-%{+YYYY.MM.dd}"
max_retries	number	N	3
node_name	string	N	
password	password	N	
port	string	N	
user	string	N	

ganglia

Ganglia is a monitoring tool that is used to monitor the performance of a cluster of machines in a distributed computing environment. Ganglia makes uses of a daemon called Gmond, which is a small service that is installed on each machine that needs to be monitored.

The `ganglia` output plugin in Logstash is used to send metrics to the `gmond` service based on events in logs.

The basic `ganglia` output plugin configuration looks like this:

```
ganglia {
    metric =>
    value =>
}
```

Configuration options

The following configuration options are available for the `ganglia` plugin

metric

The `metric` option specifies the metric that is to be used for performance monitoring. It can even take values from the event fields.

unit

The `unit` option specifies the unit like kb/s, ms for the metric used.

value

The `value` option specifies the value of metric used.

jira

The `jira` plugin doesn't come by default in Logstash installation but can be easily installed by a plugin `install` command like this:

bin/plugin install logstash-output-jira

The `jira` plugin is used to send events to a JIRA instance, which can create JIRA tickets based on certain events in your logs. To use this, the JIRA instance must accept REST API calls, since it internally makes use of JIRA REST API to pass the output events from Logstash to JIRA.

The basic configuration of the `jira` output plugin looks like this:

```
jira {
    issuetypeid =>
    password =>
    priority =>
    projectid =>
    summary =>
    username =>
}
```

Configuration options

The following are the configuration options and their corresponding data types available for the `jira` plugin:

Option	Data type	Required
assignee	string	N
issuetypeid	string	Y
password	string	Y
priority	string	Y
projectid	string	Y
reporter	string	N
summary	string	Y
username	string	Y

kafka

As explained on the Hortonworks Kafka page (`http://hortonworks.com/hadoop/kafka/`):

> *"Apache™ Kafka is a fast, scalable, durable, and fault-tolerant publish-subscribe messaging system."*

The `kafka` output plugin is used to write certain events to a topic on `kafka`. It uses the Kafka Producer API to write messages to a topic on the broker.

The basic `kafka` configuration looks like this:

```
kafka {
    topic_id =>
}
```

Configuration options

There are many `kafka` specific configuration options that can be obtained from official documentation, but the only required configuration is `topic_id`.

topic_id

The `topic_id` option defines the topic to send messages to.

lumberjack

The `lumberjack` plugin is used to write output to a Logstash forwarder or lumberjack.

The basic configuration for the `lumberjack` plugin looks like this:

```
lumberjack {
    hosts =>
    port =>
    ssl_certificate =>
}
```

Configuration options

The following configuration options are available for the `lumberjack` plugin:

hosts

The `hosts` option specifies the list of addresses where `lumberjack` can send messages to.

port

The `port` option specifies the port to connect to the `lumberjack` communication.

ssl_certificate

It specifies the path to `ssl_certificate` to be used for communication.

redis

The `redis` plugin is used to send events to a `redis` instance.

Configuration options

Configuration options are similar to the ones defined for the `redis` input plugin.

rabbitmq

 RabbitMQ is an open source message broker software (sometimes called message-oriented middleware) that implements the **Advanced Message Queuing Protocol (AMQP)**. More information is available in the official documentation at `http://www.rabbitmq.com`.

In RabbitMQ, the producer always sends messages to an exchange, and the exchange decides what to do with the messages. There are various exchange types that defines a further course of action for the messages, namely `direct`, `topic`, `headers` and `fanout`.

The `rabbitmq` plugin pushes the events from logs to the RabbitMQ exchange.

The basic configuration of the `rabbitmq` plugin looks like this:

```
rabbitmq {
    exchange =>
    exchange_type =>
    host =>
}
```

stdout

The `stdout` plugin writes the output events to the console. It is used to debug the configuration to test the event output from Logstash before integrating with other systems.

The basic configuration looks like this:

```
output {
  stdout {}
}
```

mongodb

MongoDB is a document-oriented NoSQL database, which stores data as JSON documents.

Like the `jira` plugin, this is also a community maintained plugin and doesn't ship with Logstash. It can be easily installed using the following plugin `install` command:

bin/plugin install logstash-output-mongodb

The basic configuration for the `mongodb` output plugin is:

```
mongodb {
    collection =>
    database =>
    uri =>
}
```

Configuration options

The following configuration options are available for the `mongodb` plugin:

collection

The `collection` option specifies which `mongodb` collection has to be used to write data.

database

The `database` option specifies the `mongodb` database to be used to store the data.

uri

The `uri` option specifies the connection string to be used to connect to `mongodb`.

An extensive list and latest documentation on all available Logstash output plugins is available at `https://www.elastic.co/guide/en/logstash/current/output-plugins.html`.

Filter plugins

Filter plugins are used to do intermediate processing on events read from an input plugin and before passing them as output via an output plugin. They are often used to identify the fields in input events, and to conditionally process certain parts of input events.

Let's take a look at some of the most important filter plugins.

csv

The `csv` filter is used to parse the data from an incoming CSV file and assign values to fields.

Configuration options

Configuration options for the `csv` filter plugin were covered in an example in *Chapter 2, Building Your First Data Pipeline with ELK*.

date

In ELK, it is very important to assign the correct timestamp to an event so that it can be analyzed on the `time` filter in Kibana. The `date` filter is meant to assign the appropriate timestamp based on fields in logs, or events, and assign a proper format to the timestamp.

If the `date` filter is not set, Logstash will assign a timestamp as the first time it sees the event or when the file is read.

The basic configuration of the `date` filter looks like this:

```
date {
}
```

Configuration options

Configuration options for the date filter are already covered in an example in *Chapter 2, Building Your First Data Pipeline with ELK.*

drop

The drop filter is used to drop everything that matches the conditionals for this filter.

Let's take the following instance as an example:

```
filter {
if [fieldname == "test"] {
drop {
}
}
}
```

The preceding filter will cause all events having the test fieldname to be dropped. This is very helpful to filter out non useful information out of the incoming events.

Configuration options

The following configuration options are present for this filter:

- add_field
- add_tag
- remove_field
- remove_tag

geoip

The geoip filter is used to add the geographical location of the IP address present in the incoming event. It fetches this information from the Maxmind database.

> Maxmind is a company that specializes in products built to get useful information from IP addresses. GeoIP is their IP intelligence product that is used to trace the location of an IP address. All Logstash releases have a Maxmind's GeoLite city database shipped with them. It is also available at http:// dev.maxmind.com/geoip/legacy/geolite/.

The basic configuration of the geoip filter looks like this:

```
geoip {
    source =>
}
```

Configuration options

The following configuration option is available for the `geoip` plugin.

source

The `source` option is a required setting that is of the `string` type. It is used to specify an IP address or a hostname that has to be mapped via the `geoip` service. Any field from events that contains the IP address or hostname can be provided, and if the field is of the `array` type, only the first value is taken.

grok

The `grok` option is by far the most popular and most powerful plugin that Logstash has. It can parse any unstructured log event and convert it into a structured set of fields that can be processed further and used in analysis.

It is used to parse any type of logs, whether it be apache logs, mysql logs, custom application logs, or just any unstructured text in events.

Logstash, by default, comes with a set of `grok` patterns that can be directly used to tag certain types of fields, and custom regular expressions are also supported.

All available `grok` patterns are available at:

`https://github.com/logstash-plugins/logstash-patterns-core/tree/master/patterns`

Some examples of the `grok` patterns are as follows:

```
HOSTNAME \b(?:[0-9A-Za-z][0-9A-Za-z-]{0,62})(?:\.(?:[0-9A-Za-z]
[0-9A-Za-z-]{0,62}))*(\.?|\b)
DAY (?:Mon(?:day)?|Tue(?:sday)?|Wed(?:nesday)?|Thu(?:rsday)?|Fri(?:day)?|Sat(?:urday)?|Sun(?:day)?)
YEAR (?>\d\d){1,2}
HOUR (?:2[0123]|[01]?[0-9])
MINUTE (?:[0-5][0-9])
```

The preceding `grok` patterns can be directly used to tag fields of those types with an operator like this:

```
%{HOSTNAME:host_name}
```

Here, `host_name` is the field name that we want to assign to the part of the log event that represents the hostname like `string`.

Let's try to look at `grok` in more detail:

The `grok` patterns in logs are represented by this general format:
`%{SYNTAX:SEMANTIC}`

Here, SYNTAX is the name of the pattern that matches the text in log, and SEMANTIC is the field name that we want to assign to that pattern.

Let's take the following instance as an example:

Let's say you want to represent the number of bytes transferred in one event:

```
%{NUMBER:bytes_transferred}
```

Here, bytes_transferred will refer to the actual value of bytes transferred in the log event.

Let's take a look at how we can represent a line from HTTP logs:

```
54.3.245.1 GET /index.html 14562  0.056
```

The `grok` pattern would be represented as:

```
%{IP:client_ip} %{WORD: request_method } %{URIPATHPARAM:uri_path}
%{NUMBER:bytes_transferred} %{NUMBER:duration}
```

The basic `grok` configuration for the preceding event will look like this:

```
filter{
grok{
match =>  { "message" =>"%{IP:client_ip} %{WORD:request_
method} %{URIPATHPARAM:uri_path} %{NUMBER:bytes_transferred}
%{NUMBER:duration}"}
}
}
```

After being processed with this `grok` filter, we can see the following fields added to the event with the values:

*   client_ip : 54.3.245.1
*   request_method : GET
*   uri_path :/index.html
*   bytes_transferred :14562
*   duration :0.056

Custom grok patterns

Custom `grok` patterns can be created based on a regular expression if not found in the list of `grok` patterns available.

These URLs are useful to design and test `grok` patterns for the matching text as required:

`http://grokdebug.herokuapp.com` and `http://grokconstructor.appspot.com/`

mutate

The `mutate` filter is an important filter plugin that helps rename, remove, replace, and modify fields in an incoming event. It is also specially used to convert the data type of fields, merge two fields, and convert text from lower case to upper case and vice versa.

The basic configuration of the `mutate` filter looks like this:

```
filter {
mutate {
}
}
```

Configuration options

There are various configuration options for `mutate` and most of them are understood by the name:

Option	Data type	Required	Default value
add_field	hash	N	{}
add_tag	array	N	[]
convert	hash	N	
join	hash	N	
lowercase	array	N	
merge	hash	N	
remove_field	array	N	[]
remove_tag	array	N	[]
rename	hash	N	
replace	hash	N	
split	hash	N	
strip	array	N	
update	hash	N	
uppercase	array	N	

sleep

The `sleep` option is used to put Logstash in sleep mode for the amount of time specified. We can also specify the frequency of sleep intervals based on the number of events.

Let's take the following instance as an example:

If we want to let Logstash sleep for 1 sec for every fifth event processed, we can configure it like this:

```
filter {
  sleep {
    time => "1"    # Sleep 1 second
    every => 5   # Sleep on every 5th event.
  }
}
```

An extensive list and the latest documentation on all available Logstash filter plugins is available at `https://www.elastic.co/guide/en/logstash/current/filter-plugins.html`.

Codec plugins

Codec plugins are used to encode or decode incoming or outgoing events from Logstash. They act as stream filters in input and output plugins.

Some of the most important codec plugins are:

- `avro`
- `json`
- `line`
- `multiline`
- `plain`
- `rubydebug`
- `spool`

Let's take a look at some details about some of the most commonly used ones.

json

If your input event or output event consists of full JSON documents, then the `json` codec plugin is helpful. It can be defined as:

```
input{
stdin{
```

```
codec => json{
}
}
}
```

Or it can be simply defined as:

```
input{
stdin{
codec => "json"
}
}
```

line

The `line` codec is used to read each line in an input as an event or to decode each outgoing event as a line. It can be defined as:

```
input{
stdin{
codec => line{
}
}
}
```

Or it can be simply defined as:

```
input{
stdin{
codec => "line"
}
}
```

multiline

The `multiline` codec is very helpful for certain types of events where you like to take more than one line as one event. This is really helpful in cases such as Java Exceptions or stack traces.

For example, the following configuration can take a full stack trace as one event:

```
input {
  file {
    path => "/var/log/someapp.log"
    codec => multiline {
      pattern => "^%{TIMESTAMP_ISO8601} "
      negate => true
```

```
         what => previous
      }
   }
}
```

This will take all lines that don't start with a timestamp as a part of the previous line and consider everything as a single event.

plain

The `plain` plugin is used to specify that there is no encoding or decoding required for events as it will be taken care of by corresponding input or output plugin types itself. For many plugins, such as `redis`, `mongodb` and so on, this is the default codec type.

rubydebug

The `rubydebug` plugin is used only with output event data, and it prints output event data using the Ruby Awesome Print library.

An extensive list and latest documentation on all available Logstash codec plugins is available at `https://www.elastic.co/guide/en/logstash/current/codec-plugins.html`.

Summary

In this chapter, we saw various configuration options for Logstash plugins, namely input, filter, output and codec plugins, and how these various plugins available with Logstash can be used to help collect, parse, and transform various types of events generated from multiple types of sources.

In the next chapter, we will see how we can create our own plugin to cater to the needs for custom format or to handle special type of events not handled through existing plugins.

4
Creating Custom Logstash Plugins

In the previous chapter, we saw how we could use the various available Logstash plugins for various types of input, processing and output requirements. But, if you need to create your own plugins for some custom needs, we can do that too. In this chapter, we will look at some of the following advanced concepts for Logstash plugins:

- Plugin management in Logstash.
- Downloading and installing community managed plugins.
- Creating custom Logstash plugins.

Logstash plugin management

From 1.5.0+ version onwards, Logstash plugins are separated from the core package and are maintained as separate self-contained packages using **RubyGems**. It facilitates the release of plugin updates separately from Logstash releases. Also, it reduces the overall size of the Logstash core package.

Logstash plugins are developed in Ruby.

> RubyGems is a package manager for the Ruby programming language that provides a standard format to distribute Ruby programs and libraries (in a self-contained format called a "gem"). It is a tool designed to easily manage the installation of gems, and a server to distribute them.

Logstash core plugins and community plugins are published on `https://rubygems.org/`, and can be easily downloaded from here and installed.

All Logstash plugins are stored in GitHub at the following repository:

`https://github.com/logstash-plugins`

Plugin lifecycle management

Logstash plugin management is done through the install script that is shipped with the Logstash installation:

`$LOGSTASH_HOME/bin/plugin`

Installing a plugin

To install a plugin, we can issue the following command:

`$bin/plugin install <plug_in_name>`

`plug_in_name` is the name of the plugin as mentioned in the gem name in `https://rubygems.org/` or in the Logstash plugin repository.

Let's take the following command as an example:

`$bin/plugin install logstash-input-rabbitmq`

The preceding command will install the `rabbitmq` input plugin to the Logstash installation. You can also specify the `--version` parameter to install a specific version of the plugin.

RabbitMQ (`https://www.rabbitmq.com`) is a messaging broker, a common platform to send and receive messages, which holds messages until received.

Also, plugins downloaded from `https://rubygems.org/` can be installed using the file path as follows:

`$bin/plugin install path/to/logstash-input-rabbitmq-0.1.0.gem`

You can also explore all available Logstash plugins by searching `https://rubygems.org/` for "logstash".

Plugin download page at https://rubygems.org/

Updating a plugin

To update a previously installed plugin, we can issue the command:

```
$bin/plugin update <plug_in_name>
```

Let's take the following command as an example:

```
$bin/plugin update logstash-input-rabbitmq
```

The preceding command will update the `logstash-input-rabbitmq` plugin to the latest version. Please make sure to test the updates well before moving on to the production environment.

Uninstalling a plugin

To uninstall a plugin, we can issue the following command:

```
$bin/plugin uninstall <plug_in_name>
```

Let's take the following command as an example:

```
$bin/plugin uninstall logstash-input-rabbitmq
```

The preceding command will uninstall the `logstash-input-rabbitmq` plugin from the Logstash installation.

Structure of a Logstash plugin

As already mentioned in Logstash plugin management, Logstash plugins are self-contained RubyGems.

 This section requires a little bit knowledge of the Ruby programming language. If you are looking for a quick overview, you can look at the official Ruby tutorial here:

`https://www.ruby-lang.org/en/documentation/quickstart/`

As extensive knowledge of Ruby is not expected from the readers, we will take a look at some simple illustrations of how a plugin works, and how we can design one simple plugin on our own. We will also cover some details of how the plugins are bundled to gems. More information is available at `https://www.elastic.co/guide/en/logstash/current/contributing-to-logstash.html`.

Let's look at the structure of a `drop filter` plugin, which is used to drop certain events on certain conditions (`https://github.com/logstash-plugins/logstash-filter-drop`):

```
# encoding: utf-8
require "logstash/filters/base"
require "logstash/namespace"

# Drop filter.
#
# Drops everything that gets to this filter.
#
# This is best used in combination with conditionals, for example:
# [source,ruby]
#     filter {
#       if [loglevel] == "debug" {
#         drop { }
#       }
#     }
#
# The above will only pass events to the drop filter if the loglevel
field is
# `debug`. This will cause all events matching to be dropped.
class LogStash::Filters::Drop < LogStash::Filters::Base
```

```
config_name "drop"
# Drop all the events within a pre-configured percentage.
#
# This is useful if you just need a percentage but not the whole.
#
# Example, to only drop around 40% of the events that have the field
loglevel wiht value "debug".
#
#      filter {
#        if [loglevel] == "debug" {
#          drop {
#            percentage => 40
#          }
#        }
#      }
config :percentage, :validate => :number, :default => 100
public
def register
  # nothing to do.
end

public
def filter(event)
  event.cancel if (@percentage == 100 || rand < (@percentage /
100.0))
end # def filter
end # class LogStash::Filters::Drop
```

Now, let's try to break it down and look at each component of a plugin.

Required dependencies

The first requirement actually loads the `logstash/namespace.rb` file, which defines the modules namespaces for the input, filter, output, and codec plugins.

```
require "logstash/namespace"
```

Then, since this is a `filter` plugin, we will add dependency for the filter:

```
require "logstash/filters/base"
```

Similarly, for input, we can add `/logstash/inputs/base`, and for output `/logstash/outputs/base`.

Class declaration

Next, for each plugin, we need to declare a class for it, and it should include the required `Base` class for the `filter` plugin as well:

```
class LogStash::Filters::Drop < LogStash::Filters::Base
```

So, as we have a `drop` filter, we will declare a class by its name.

Configuration name

Next, we need to specify the name of the plugin that will be used in the Logstash configuration. We do this by declaring `config_name`:

```
config_name "drop"
```

So, it will be used like this:

```
filter {
drop {
}
}
```

Configuration options setting

We can define as many configuration options as we need for the plugin with this setting. It allows us to set the name of the option, its data type and default value, and specify if it is required:

```
config :percentage, :validate => :number, :default => 100
```

The following are the configurations:

- `:validate`: It allows us to enforce the data type for the option. The possible values can be `:string`, `:number`, `:array`, `:hash`, `:boolean`, and so on.

  For the `drop` filter, we have a specified validation for the `percentage` option to be of type `:number`.

- `:default`: It allows us to specify the default value for the option.

  For the `drop` filter, we have specified the value `100` as the default for the option named `percentage`.

- `:required`: It takes a boolean value as either `true` or `false` and specifies whether the option is required or not.

Plugin methods

Every plugin type (input, filter, output, and codec) has certain methods that they need to implement to initialize instance variables and to execute actual operations inside the plugin.

Plugin type	Methods
Input plugin	`register` and `run`(queue)
Filter plugin	`register` and `filter`(event)
Output plugin	`register` and `receive`
Codec plugin	`register`, `encode`, `decode`

Input plugin

For the input plugin, the `register` and `run`(queue) methods need to be implemented.

The `register` method is used to initialize the instance variables if any.

The `run` method converts the stream of incoming messages to events that can be further transformed:

```
public
def run(queue)
  #Code which converts messages to event here.
end # def run
```

Filter plugin

For the filter plugin, the `register` and `filter` (event) methods need to be implemented:

```
public
def register
  # nothing to do.
end
```

The `register` method is used to initialize instance variables if any. For `drop` filter, we don't need to use any instance variables, so we will keep it empty.

```
public
def filter(event)
  event.cancel if (@percentage == 100 || rand < (@percentage /
100.0))
end # def filter
```

The `filter` method does the actual work of filtering the events. Inside the `filter` method, we can use the `config` parameters set using an `'@'` prefix, and we have event properties available using event `hashmap`.

For example, we can get the message as event `["message"]`.

Also, certain operations, such as event `.cancel`, are also available.

For example, in the `drop` filter, we will use event `.cancel` to cancel the event matching this filter.

Output plugin

For the output plugin, the `register` and `receive` methods need to be implemented.

The `register` method is used to initialize the instance variables, if any.

The `receive` method processes the events before sending them to the output destination, depending on the type of plugin.

```
public
def receive(event)
end # def event
```

Codec plugin

The codec plugin is used with input and output plugins to decode an input event or encoding an outgoing event.

For the codec plugin, `register`, `encode` or `decode` methods need to be implemented.

The `register` method is used to initialize instance variables, if any.

The `encode` method is used to encode an event to another format.

An example is the `json` codec plugin, which transforms the events to `json` format:

```
public
  def encode(event)
    @on_event.call(event, event.to_json)
  end
```

The `decode` method decodes the incoming data to an event. This method needs a `yield` statement to return decoded events to a pipeline.

For example, in the `spool` codec plugin, to send the messages to some buffer:

```
  public
def decode(data)
  data.each do |event|
    yield event
  end
end
```

Writing a Logstash filter plugin

Now, we have seen the structure of a plugin, which gives us a head start on developing one of our own.

In this section, we will demonstrate building a simple filter plugin using the knowledge of the structure of a plugin that we acquired in the previous section.

In this illustration, we will assume that we have a sequence of numbers coming in a stream, and we want to denote them with certain currencies based on a name, which we will pass as a parameter to the plugin. Let's see what our simple `currency` filter plugin looks like:

```
# Adds a Currency Symbol to price field
#
#filter {
#    currency{
#        name => "$"
#    }
#}

require "logstash/filters/base"
require "logstash/namespace"

class LogStash::Filters::Currency < LogStash::Filters::Base

config_name "currency"

config :name, :validate => :string, :default => "$"

public
def register
#do nothing
end

public
```

```
def filter(event)
    if @name
        msg = @name + event["message"]
        event["message"] = msg
    end
end

end
```

Let's take a look at how the preceding filter is structured.

First, we have added the dependency for the required classes:

```
require "logstash/filters/base"
require "logstash/namespace"
```

Then, we have defined a class for the filter:

```
class LogStash::Filters::Currency < LogStash::Filters::Base
```

Next, we named the filter using `config_name`:

```
config_name "currency"
```

Now, we will specify the configuration option needed for this filter as we need the name of the currency to be specified so we can add it to the message. We will define it as follows:

```
config :name, :validate => :string, :default => "$"
```

Then, as we don't need to set any instance variables, we have provided an empty `register` method for the filter:

```
public
def register
#do nothing
end
```

Next, we will implement the `filter` method for the `filter` plugin, which will take an event and apply the logic for `currency`:

```
public
def filter(event)
    if @name
        msg = @name + event["message"]
        event["message"] = msg
    end
end
```

Here, we will first check the value of the `name` filter and if it is present, we will add the value in front of the message; otherwise, the filter will be ignored.

Now, `filter` can be used as follows:

```
filter {
    currency{
        name => "$"
    }
}
```

Let's say if your input is `200` after using this filter, each incoming event's output from the Logstash filter plugin will look like this:

```
{

"@timestamp" => "2015-06-21T14:21:54.123Z",
"message" => "$200",
}
```

Building the plugin

Now, when we have successfully created a plugin, save it as `currency.rb` in the following folder structure:

```
logstash-filter-currency
└──lib
|      └──logstash
|           └──filters
|      └──currency.rb
Gemfile
logstash-filter-currency.gemspec
```

Now, to create the RubyGem for the folder, we will require a gemfile and a gemspec file present in the `logstash-filter-currency` top folder.

> **gemfile**: A gemfile describes the gem dependencies required to execute associated Ruby code.
>
> **gemspec file**: A gemspec file defines the specification of the RubyGem that will be built.

Let's add some specifications to our gemspec file:

```
Gem::Specification.new do |s|
    s.name = 'logstash-filter-currency'
    s.version        = '0.1.0'
    s.licenses = ['Apache License (2.0)']
    s.summary = "This plugin adds a currency name before message."
    s.description = "This plugin is used to add core logstash available
plugin, to define a new functionality of adding currency
symbols for certain messages"
    s.authors = ["Saurabh Chhajed"]
    s.email = 'saurabh.chhajed@gmail.com'
    s.homepage = "http://saurzcode.in"
    s.require_paths = ["lib"]

    # Files
    s.files = ["lib/logstash/filters/currency.rb"]


    # Special flag to let us know this is actually a logstash plugin
    s.metadata = { "logstash_plugin" => "true", "logstash_group" =>
"filter" }

    # Gem dependencies
    s.add_runtime_dependency "logstash-core", '>= 1.4.0', '< 2.0.0'
    s.add_development_dependency 'logstash-devutils'
end
```

Save this `logstash-filter-currency.gemspec` file under the root plugin folder as shown in the folder structure.

It requires Ruby gem bundlers to build gems based on these files, which can be easily installed on the Ruby console using:

```
$ gem install bundler
```

More information on using bundler can be found at `http://bundler.io/`.

Now, we can build the gem using:

```
$gem build logstash-filter-currency.gemspec
```

That's it! This should have created a gem named `logstash-filter-currency-0.1.0.gem` in the same folder.

It can be installed to the existing Logstash installation easily:

```
$ bin/plugin install /path/to/ logstash-filter-currency-0.1.0.gem
```

If successful, you should see the plugin listed in:

```
$bin/plugin list
```

We can quickly test the plugin using the `logstash -e` flag option:

```
bin/logstash -e 'input { stdin{} } filter { currency {  name => "$" } }
output {stdout { codec => rubydebug }}'
```

For the `filter` plugin, any number that we write will be appended by the $ currency name:

```
200
{
        "message" => "$200"
        "@version" => "1",
        "@timestamp" => "2015-06-27T19:17:20.230Z",
        "host" => "saurzcode"
}
```

We can see $ being added to the number `200` that we entered as standard input.

Now, we have successfully created our first Logstash filter plugin and tested it successfully.

Similarly, plugins of input and output types can be created and deployed.

Summary

In this chapter, we saw how to create a custom Logstash plugin for requirements that were not fulfilled through the available plugins. By now, we've seen all the different types of features and plugins supported by Logstash and how we can extend Logstash for varying needs of input and output sources.

Next, we will take a detailed look at the features of the other two components of ELK stack — Elasticsearch, and Kibana.

5
Why Do We Need Elasticsearch in ELK?

In this chapter, we will look at the role of Elasticsearch in ELK Stack. It covers the features of Elasticsearch, and why it is such a wonderful technology to enable fast search responses for real time analytics. In the end, we will also briefly look at some of the plugins available for Elasticsearch, which make our lives much easier while dealing with the Elasticsearch cluster.

Why Elasticsearch?

Elasticsearch is a search and analytics engine that enables fast and scalable searches in a distributed environment. As we have already covered in *Chapter 1, Introduction to ELK Stack*, some of the biggest distributed architectures, such as GitHub, StackOverflow, and Wikipedia, make use of the Elasticsearch full-text search, structured search, and analytics capabilities for fast and relevant searches.

Elasticsearch is built on Apache Lucene. The definition of Lucene from its Apache page (https://lucene.apache.org) is:

> *"Apache LuceneTM is a high-performance, full-featured text search engine library written entirely in Java. It is a technology suitable for nearly any application that requires full-text search, especially cross-platform"*

Elasticsearch hides the complexity behind Lucene by providing a powerful RESTful API built on top of it, which makes querying the indexed data easier, and makes it available to any programming language. It extends the capabilities of Lucene by providing real-time analytics built on structured and unstructured data of petabytes of size distributed across many servers.

Before taking a deep dive into the various APIs that Elasticsearch provides, let's understand some of the basic concepts of Elasticsearch.

Elasticsearch basic concepts

Let's look at some of the basic concepts of Elasticsearch, which explain how it stores the indexed data.

Index

Index in Elasticsearch is a collection of documents that share some common characteristics.

Each index contains multiple types, which in turn contains multiple documents, and each document contains multiple fields. An index consists of multiple JSON documents in Elasticsearch. There can be any number of indices in a cluster in Elasticsearch.

In ELK, when Logstash JSON documents are sent to Elasticsearch, they are sent as the default index pattern `"logstash-%{+YYYY.MM.dd}"`. It partitions indices by day so that it can easily be searched and deleted if required. This pattern can be changed in the Logstash output plugin configuration.

The URL to search and query the indices looks like this:

```
http://localhost:9200/[index]/[type]/[operation]
```

Document

A document in Elasticsearch is a JSON document stored in an index. Each document has a type and corresponding ID, which represents it uniquely.

For example, a document stored in Elasticsearch would look similar to this:

```
{
  "_index" : "packtpub",
  "_type" : "elk",
  "_id" : "1",
  "_version" : 1,
  "found" : true,
  "_source":{
book_name : "learning elk"
}
}
```

Field

A field is a basic unit inside a document. As in the preceding example, a basic field is a key value pair as follows:

```
book_name : "learning elk"
```

Type

Type is used to provide a logical partition inside the indices. It basically represents a class of similar types of documents. An index can have multiple types and we can define them as per the context.

For example, the index for Facebook can have `post` as one of the index types, `comments` as another.

Mapping

Mapping is used to map each field of the document with its corresponding data type, such as `string`, `integer`, `float`, `double`, `date`, and so on. Elasticsearch creates a mapping for the fields automatically during index creation, and those mappings can be easily queried or modified based on specific types of needs.

Shard

A shard is the actual physical entity where the data for each index is stored. Each index can have a number of primary and replica shards where it stores the data. Shards are distributed among all the nodes in the cluster and can be moved from one node to another in case of node failures or the addition of new nodes.

Primary shard and replica shard

Each document in an Elasticsearch index is stored on one primary shard and a number of replica shards. While indexing, the document is first stored on a primary shard and then on the corresponding replica shard. By default, the number of primary shards for each index is five and can be configured as per our needs.

Replica shards will typically reside on a different node than the primary shard and help in case of failover and load balancing to cater to multiple requests.

Cluster

A cluster is a collection of nodes that stores the indexed data. Elasticsearch provides horizontal scalability with the help of data stored in the cluster. Each cluster is represented by a cluster name, which different nodes join. The cluster name is set by a property called `cluster.name` in the Elasticsearch configuration `elasticsearch.yml`, which defaults to `"elasticsearch"`:

```
cluster.name: elasticsearch
```

Node

A node is a single running instance of Elasticsearch, which belongs to one of the clusters. By default, every node in Elasticsearch joins the cluster named "elasticsearch". Each node can have its own configuration defined in elasticsearch.yml, they can have different settings regarding memory and resource allocations.

In Elasticsearch, nodes can play three types of roles:

- **Data node**: Data nodes index documents and perform searches on indexed documents. It is always recommended to add more data nodes in order to increase performance or scale the cluster. A node can be made a data node by setting these properties in the elasticsearch.yml configuration for the node:

```
node.master = false
node.data=true
```

- **Master node**: Master nodes are responsible for management of a cluster. For large clusters, it is recommended to have three dedicated master nodes (one primary and two backup), which only act as master nodes and do not store indices or perform searches. A node can be configured to be a dedicated master node with this configuration in elasticsearch.yml:

```
node.master =true
node.data=false
```

- **Routing node or load balancer node**: These nodes do not play the role of either a master or data node, but just perform load balancing, or routing of requests for searches, or indexing the document to appropriate nodes. This is useful for high volume searches or index operations. A node can be configured to be a routing node with this configuration in elasticsearch.yml:

```
node.master =false
node.data=false
```

Exploring the Elasticsearch API

In ELK, although Logstash and Kibana act as an interface to talk to Elasticsearch indices, it's still necessary to understand how Logstash and Kibana makes use of Elasticsearch RESTful APIs to perform various operations, such as creating and managing indices, storing and retrieving the documents, and forming various types of search queries around the indices. It is also often useful to know how to delete indices.

As we already know, Elasticsearch provides an extensive API to perform various operations. The generic syntax of querying the cluster from the command line is as follows:

```
$curl -X<VERB>
'<PROTOCOL>://<HOST>:<PORT>/<PATH>/<OPERATION_NAME>?<QUERY_STRING>' -
d '<BODY>'
```

Let's understand various parts of this command:

- VERB: This can take values for the request method type: GET, POST, PUT, DELETE, HEAD.

- PROTOCOL: This is either http or https.

- HOST: This is the hostname of the node in the cluster. For local installations, this can be 'localhost' or '127.0.0.1'.

- PORT: This is the port on which the Elasticsearch instance is currently running. The default is 9200.

- PATH: This corresponds to the name of the index, type, and ID to be queried, for example: /index/type/id.

- OPERATION_NAME: This corresponds to the name of the operation to be performed, for example: _search, _count, and so on.

- QUERY_STRING: This is an optional parameter to be specified for query string parameters. For example, ?pretty for pretty print of JSON documents.

- BODY: This makes a request for body text.

Let's take the following command as an example:

```
curl -XGET 'http://localhost:9200/logstash-2014.08.04/_search?pretty'
```

This URL will search in the index named logstash-2014.08.04.

For the upcoming sections, it is assumed that you have already installed Elasticsearch as explained in *Chapter 1, Introduction to ELK Stack*, and it is running.

In this section, we will make use of the indices created in our example in *Chapter 2, Building Your First Data Pipeline with ELK*, and will try to perform some operations on them.

Listing all available indices

Let's first try to see all available indices in our cluster by executing the following command:

```
curl -XGET 'localhost:9200/_cat/indices?v'
```

Upon executing this, we will get the following response:

```
health status index                  pri rep docs.count docs.deleted store.
size pri.store.size
green  open   logstash-2014.12.19      5   1          1            0
6.1kb           6.1kb
green  open   logstash-2014.12.08      5   1          1            0
6.1kb           6.1kb
green  open   logstash-2014.07.17      5   1          1            0
6kb              6kb
green  open   logstash-2014.08.04      5   1          1            0
6.1kb           6.1kb
green  open   logstash-2014.11.05      5   1          1            0
6.1kb           6.1kb
green  open   logstash-2014.07.27      5   1          1            0
6.1kb           6.1kb
green  open   logstash-2014.09.16      5   1          1            0
6.1kb           6.1kb
green  open   logstash-2014.12.15      5   1          1            0
6.1kb           6.1kb
green  open   logstash-2014.12.10      5   1          1            0
6.1kb           6.1kb
green  open   logstash-2014.09.18      5   1          1            0
6kb              6kb
green  open   logstash-2014.12.18      5   1          1            0
6.1kb           6.1kb
green  open   logstash-2014.07.08      5   1          1            0
6.1kb           6.1kb
```

This will show all the indices that are stored among all nodes in the cluster, and some information about them such as health, index name, size, count of documents, number of primary shards, and so on.

For example, the first row in the preceding text shows that we have 5 primary and 1 replica shards of the index named logstash-2014.12.19 and it has 1 document in it and 0 deleted documents.

Listing all nodes in a cluster

We can also see all nodes in a cluster by invoking the following command:

```
curl -XGET  'http://localhost:9200/_cat/nodes?v'
```

The response is as follows:

```
host       ip            heap.percent   ram.percent load node.role
master name
packtpub 127.0.1.1           18            35         0.27    d
*       Animus
```

Since ours is a single node cluster on `localhost`, it shows one node and the memory related characteristics of this node.

Checking the health of the cluster

We can check the health of a cluster by invoking the following command:

```
curl -XGET 'http://localhost:9200/_cluster/health?pretty=true'
{
  "cluster_name" : "elasticsearch",
  "status" : "yellow",
  "timed_out" : false,
  "number_of_nodes" : 1,
  "number_of_data_nodes" : 1,
  "active_primary_shards" : 11,
  "active_shards" : 11,
  "relocating_shards" : 0,
  "initializing_shards" : 0,
  "unassigned_shards" : 11
}
```

Health can be checked at cluster level, shard level, or indices level, using URLs that are similar to the following ones:

```
curl -XGET 'http://localhost:9200/_cluster/health?level=cluster&pretty=true'
curl -XGET 'http://localhost:9200/_cluster/health?level=shards&pretty=true'
curl -XGET 'http://localhost:9200/_cluster/health?level=indices&pretty=true'
```

Health status of the cluster

Elasticsearch cluster health is indicated in three parameters:

- **Red** indicates that some or all primary shards are not ready to serve the requests.

- **Yellow** indicates that all primary shards are allocated but some or all of the replicas have not been allocated. Normally, single node clusters will have their health status as yellow as no other node is available for replication.

- **Green** indicates that all shards and their replicas are well allocated and the cluster is fully operational.

Creating an index

In ELK, index creation is automatically handled by providing the index name in the Logstash `elasticsearch` output plugin. Still, let's take a look at how we can create an index:

```
curl -XPUT 'localhost:9200/<index_name>?pretty'
```

For example, to create an index named `packtpub`, we can issue the following command:

```
curl -XPUT 'localhost:9200/packtpub/?pretty'
```

We can also directly create an index while putting the document inside the index as follows:

```
curl -xPUT 'localhost:9200/packtpub/elk/1?pretty' -d '
{
book_name : "learning elk"
}'
```

The response of the preceding command is:

```
{
  "_index" : "packtpub",
  "_type" : "elk",
  "_id" : "1",
  "_version" : 1,
  "created" : true
}
```

With the preceding command, a new index named `packtpub` was created along with type `elk`, and a document with ID `1` was stored in it.

Retrieving the document

We will now retrieve the document that we just indexed:

```
curl -XGET 'localhost:9200/packtpub/elk/1?pretty'
```

The response of the preceding query will be:

```
{
  "_index" : "packtpub",
  "_type" : "elk",
  "_id" : "1",
  "_version" : 1,
  "found" : true,
  "_source":{
 book_name : "learning elk"
 }
 }
```

The _source field will contain a full document, which was indexed with ID as 1.

From our GOOG price indices example from *Chapter 2, Building Your First Data Pipeline with ELK*, let's try to query for a document:

```
curl -XGET 'localhost:9200/logstash-2014.08.04/logs/_search?pretty'
```

This will give us the following response:

```
{
  "took" : 3,
  "timed_out" : false,
  "_shards" : {
    "total" : 5,
    "successful" : 5,
    "failed" : 0
  },
  "hits" : {
    "total" : 1,
    "max_score" : 1.0,
    "hits" : [ {
      "_index" : "logstash-2014.08.04",
      "_type" : "logs",
      "_id" : "AU2qgZixPoayDyQnreXd",
      "_score" : 1.0,
```

```
        "_source":{"message":["2014-08-05,570.05255,571.9826,562.61255,
565.07257,1551200,565.07257"],"@version":"1","@timestamp":"2014-08-
04T23:00:00.000Z","host":"packtpub","path":"/opt/logstash/input/
GOOG.csv","date_of_record":"2014-08-05","open":570.05255,"high":5
71.9826,"low":562.61255,"close":565.07257,"volume":1551200,"adj_
close":"565.07257"}
      } ]
    }
}
```

We got the complete message stored as the _source field, which contains JSON emitted from Logstash.

Deleting documents

In order to delete a document inside one index, we can issue the following command:

```
curl -XDELETE 'localhost:9200/packtpub/elk/1?pretty'
```

Deleting an index

Let's delete the index that we created:

```
curl -XDELETE 'localhost:9200/packtpub?pretty'
```

The response is as follows:

```
{
  "acknowledged" : true
}
```

This indicates that the index was successfully deleted.

Elasticsearch Query DSL

The queries that we saw until now were basic commands that were used to retrieve data, but the actual power of Elasticsearch's querying lies in a robust Query Domain Specific Language based on JSON also called Query DSL. Kibana makes extensive use of Query DSL in order to get results in a desired format for you. You almost never really have to worry about writing the query JSON, as Kibana will automatically create and put the results in a nice format.

For example, in order to get only three results out of all the matching ones, we can specify it like this:

```
curl -XPOST 'localhost:9200/logstash-*/_search' -d '
{
  "query": { "match_all": {} },
  "size": 3
}'
```

The response is as follows, which contains three documents matching the search:

```
{
    "took" : 390,
    "timed_out" : false,
    "_shards" : {
      "total" : 640,
      "successful" : 640,
      "failed" : 0
    },
    "hits" : {
      "total" : 128,
      "max_score" : 1.0,
      "hits" : [{
          "_index" : "logstash-2014.07.01",
          "_type" : "logs",
          "_id" : "AU2qge3cPoayDyQnreX0",
          "_score" : 1.0,
          "_source" : {
            "message" : ["2014-07-
02,583.3526,585.44269,580.39264,582.33765,1056400,582.33765"],
            "@version" : "1",
            "@timestamp" : "2014-07-01T23:00:00.000Z",
            "host" : "packtpub",
            "path" : "/opt/logstash/input/GOOG.csv",
            "date_of_record" : "2014-07-02",
            "open" : 583.3526,
            "high" : 585.44269,
            "low" : 580.39264,
            "close" : 582.33765,
            "volume" : 1056400,
            "adj_close" : "582.33765"
          }
        }, {
          "_index" : "logstash-2014.07.09",
```

```
        "_type" : "logs",
        "_id" : "AU2qge3cPoayDyQnreXv",
        "_score" : 1.0,
        "_source" : {
          "message" : ["2014-07-
10,565.91254,576.59265,565.01257,571.10254,1356700,571.10254"],
          "@version" : "1",
          "@timestamp" : "2014-07-09T23:00:00.000Z",
          "host" : "packtpub",
          "path" : "/opt/logstash/input/GOOG.csv",
          "date_of_record" : "2014-07-10",
          "open" : 565.91254,
          "high" : 576.59265,
          "low" : 565.01257,
          "close" : 571.10254,
          "volume" : 1356700,
          "adj_close" : "571.10254"
        }
      }, {
        "_index" : "logstash-2014.07.21",
        "_type" : "logs",
        "_id" : "AU2qgZixPoayDyQnreXn",
        "_score" : 1.0,
        "_source" : {
          "message" : ["2014-07-
22,590.72266,599.65271,590.60266,594.74268,1699200,594.74268"],
          "@version" : "1",
          "@timestamp" : "2014-07-21T23:00:00.000Z",
          "host" : "packtpub",
          "path" : "/opt/logstash/input/GOOG.csv",
          "date_of_record" : "2014-07-22",
          "open" : 590.72266,
          "high" : 599.65271,
          "low" : 590.60266,
          "close" : 594.74268,
          "volume" : 1699200,
          "adj_close" : "594.74268"
        }
      }
    ]
  }
}
```

Similarly, the query to get results sorted by a field will look similar to this:

```
curl -XPOST 'localhost:9200/logstash-*/_search' -d '
{
"query" : {
"match_all" :{}
},
"sort" : {"open" : { "order":"desc"}},
"size" :3
}'
```

You can see the response of the preceding query, sorted by the "open" field in a desc manner:

```
{
    "took" : 356,
    "timed_out" : false,
    "_shards" : {
      "total" : 640,
      "successful" : 640,
      "failed" : 0
    },
    "hits" : {
      "total" : 128,
      "max_score" : null,
      "hits" : [{
          "_index" : "logstash-2014.07.23",
          "_type" : "logs",
          "_id" : "AU2qgZixPoayDyQnreXl",
          "_score" : null,
          "_source" : {
            "message" : ["2014-07-
24,596.4527,599.50269,591.77271,593.35266,1035100,593.35266"],
            "@version" : "1",
            "@timestamp" : "2014-07-23T23:00:00.000Z",
            "host" : "packtpub",
            "path" : "/opt/logstash/input/GOOG.csv",
            "date_of_record" : "2014-07-24",
            "open" : 596.4527,
            "high" : 599.50269,
            "low" : 591.77271,
            "close" : 593.35266,
            "volume" : 1035100,
```

```
            "adj_close" : "593.35266"
          },
          "sort" : [596.4527]
        }, {
          "_index" : "logstash-2014.09.21",
          "_type" : "logs",
          "_id" : "AU2qgZioPoayDyQnreW8",
          "_score" : null,
          "_source" : {
            "message" : ["2014-09-
22,593.82269,593.95166,583.46271,587.37262,1689500,587.37262"],
            "@version" : "1",
            "@timestamp" : "2014-09-21T23:00:00.000Z",
            "host" : "packtpub",
            "path" : "/opt/logstash/input/GOOG.csv",
            "date_of_record" : "2014-09-22",
            "open" : 593.82269,
            "high" : 593.95166,
            "low" : 583.46271,
            "close" : 587.37262,
            "volume" : 1689500,
            "adj_close" : "587.37262"
          },
          "sort" : [593.82269]
        }, {
          "_index" : "logstash-2014.07.22",
          "_type" : "logs",
          "_id" : "AU2qgZixPoayDyQnreXm",
          "_score" : null,
          "_source" : {
            "message" : ["2014-07-
23,593.23267,597.85266,592.50269,595.98267,1233200,595.98267"],
            "@version" : "1",
            "@timestamp" : "2014-07-22T23:00:00.000Z",
            "host" : "packtpub",
            "path" : "/opt/logstash/input/GOOG.csv",
            "date_of_record" : "2014-07-23",
            "open" : 593.23267,
            "high" : 597.85266,
            "low" : 592.50269,
            "close" : 595.98267,
            "volume" : 1233200,
            "adj_close" : "595.98267"
          },
```

```
            "sort" : [593.23267]
        }
    ]
  }
}
```

More details on Query DSL can be found at the Elasticsearch
official documentation here:

```
https://www.elastic.co/guide/en/elasticsearch/
reference/current/query-dsl.html
```

Now when we have an understanding of Query DSL in Elasticsearch, let's look at
one of the queries automatically created by Kibana, in our example from *Chapter 2,
Building Your First Data Pipeline with ELK*.

Go to the Kibana **Visualize** page and open the *Highest Traded Volume Visualization*
that we created earlier. If we click on the arrow button at the bottom, it opens up
buttons for **Request**, **Response** like this:

Elasticsearch Request Body on Kibana UI

Here, we can easily see the request sent by Kibana to Elasticsearch as **Elasticsearch request body**:

```
{
  "query": {
    "filtered": {
      "query": {
        "query_string": {
          "analyze_wildcard": true,
          "query": "*"
        }
      },
      "filter": {
        "bool": {
          "must": [
            {
              "range": {
                "@timestamp": {
                  "gte": 1403880285618,
                  "lte": 1419472695417
                }
              }
            }
          ],
          "must_not": []
        }
      }
    }
  },
  "size": 0,
  "aggs": {
    "1": {
      "max": {
        "field": "volume"
      }
    }
  }
}
```

The preceding query makes use of query filters to apply range on the `@timestamp` field, along with aggregations to find the maximum value of the `"Volume"` field. Similarly, we can also check for other visualizations created. Kibana takes care of creating queries for all the types of visualizations that you create.

Elasticsearch plugins

Elasticsearch has a very rich set of plugins, mainly community driven, which are really helpful to analyze the cluster, and execute full-text structural queries easily.

Let's look at a few of the plugins.

Bigdesk plugin

This plugin was developed by Lukas Vlcek. It helps analyze the nodes across the cluster with the help of live charts and various statistics related to JVM, CPU, and OS, and about shards and their replicas.

> More information is available at `https://github.com/lukas-vlcek/bigdesk`.

The following screenshot shows the Bigdesk plugin:

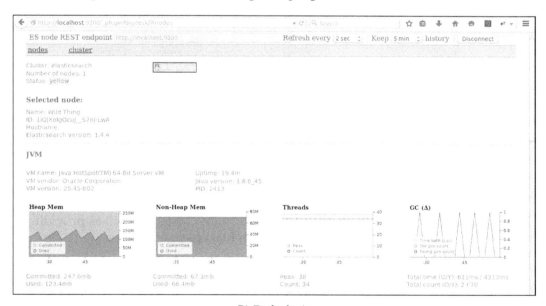

BigDesk plugin

Elastic-Hammer plugin

The Elastic-Hammer plugin acts as a frontend for Elasticsearch. It helps query the cluster and provides syntax checking while typing queries as well.

 More details can be found here: `https://github.com/andrewvc/elastic-hammer`.

Elasticsearch Elastic-Hammer plugin

Head plugin

Head plugins are capable of generating statistics of the cluster, as well as providing browsing, and performing structured queries on Elasticsearch indices.

 More details can be found here: `https://github.com/mobz/elasticsearch-head`.

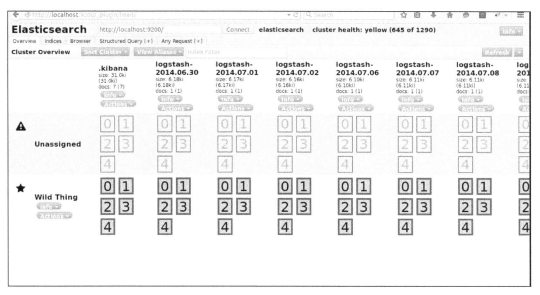

Elasticsearch head plugin

There are many more plugins available that are supported by Elasticsearch or by the community and they play an important role while interacting with Elasticsearch.

You can easily check the list of available plugins here:

https://www.elastic.co/guide/en/elasticsearch/
reference/current/modules-plugins.html#_plugins

Summary

In this chapter, we learned the basic concepts of Elasticsearch. We also figured out how querying on a Elasticsearch index works, and how Kibana makes use of Elasticsearch queries to efficiently analyze indexed data and show beautiful visualizations on top of it.

In the next chapter, we will look at Kibana's features in more detail to understand how it helps perform some searches on data with querying on its **Discover** page.

6

Finding Insights with Kibana

In the previous chapter, we saw how Elasticsearch plays a role in ELK Stack to support fast searches and a variety of aggregations. In this chapter, we will take a look at how Kibana acts as the frontend of ELK, where it hides all the complexities of data and presents beautiful visualizations, charts, and dashboards built over the data, which helps gain essential insights into the data.

Kibana makes it easy to create and share dashboards consisting of various types of charts and graphs. Kibana visualizations automatically display changes in data over time based on Elasticsearch queries. It's easy to install and set up, and helps us quickly explore and discover many aspects of data.

Kibana 4 features

Some of the unique features in Kibana 4 are as follows:

Search highlights

Search terms are highlighted in the list of documents shown after the search:

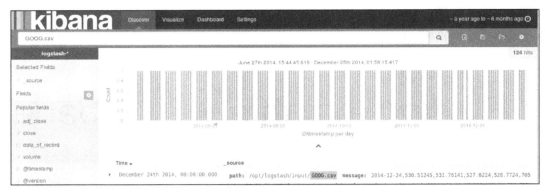

Search highlight in Kibana 4

Elasticsearch aggregations

Kibana 4 makes extensive use of Elasticsearch aggregations and sub aggregations to provide more than one aggregation for visualizations. There are mainly two types of aggregations — Bucketing and Metrics. Bucketing produces a list of buckets, each one with a set of documents belonging to it, for example, terms, range, histograms, and so on. Metrics calculate the compute metrics for a set of documents, for example, min, max, sum, average, and so on. These types of computations can only be done on numeric type of fields.

Scripted fields

Scripted fields are used to make computations on the fly on indexed data.
For example, for a certain field you always want to multiply by `100` before you show it. You can save it as a scripted field. Scripted fields, though, can't be searched.

Let's take the following script as an example: `doc['volume'].value * 100`.

This script will always multiply the value of volume by `100` before it shows it.

Dynamic dashboards

Dashboards are very flexible and dynamic as individual visualizations can be easily arranged as per convenience, and data can be refreshed automatically.

Kibana interface

A Kibana interface consists of four main tabs:

- **Discover**: The **Discover** page enables free text searches, field-based searches, range-based searches, and so on.
- **Visualize**: The **Visualize** page enables building many visualizations, such as pie charts, bar charts, line charts, and so on, which can be saved and used in dashboards later.
- **Dashboard**: The **Dashboard** represents collections of multiple visualizations and searches, which can be used to easily apply filters based on click interaction, and draw conclusions based on multiple data aggregations.
- **Settings**: **Settings** enables the configuration of index patterns, scripted fields, the data types of fields, and so on.

Let's take a look at the **Discover** page in more detail.

Discover page

The **Discover** page is used to perform interactive searches on your indexed data. It allows you to perform ad hoc searches based on fields, the filtering of data, and allows you to view indexed documents as well.

A typical Kibana home page, which defaults to the **Discover** page, looks as follows:

Kibana Discover page

The **Discover** page shows all the indexed fields in the **Index Pattern** on the left, a **Time Filter** at the top, and a **Search Box** to enter your search queries. Also, it shows a default **Histogram** based on the **@timestamp** field in the documents and displays **No. of Hits** in the document corresponding to your search. It shows **500** documents by default with the latest based on the timestamp at the top.

Time filter

Remember the time when your boss asked to find some statistics from your data for a specific time? The time filter is the answer for these kinds of searches. You can filter data on any specific time period selected from the calendar, called **Absolute**, or make it **Relative** based on current time. There are also some quick time filters available for use.

Quick time filter

A quick time filter helps filter quickly based on some already available time ranges:

Kibana Time Filter – Quick

Relative time filter

A relative time filter helps filter based on relative time from the current time. By default, the time filter is set to **Relative** with **15 Minutes ago** from **Now**:

Kibana Time Filter - Relative

Absolute time filter

The absolute time filter helps filter based on a range of dates selected for **From** and **To** a date and time:

Kibana Time Filter – Absolute

Kibana Auto-refresh setting

The **Auto-refresh** setting can be set to set a refresh interval:

Kibana Auto-refresh setting

The time filter can also be specified using click and drag on an area of a histogram or other charts:

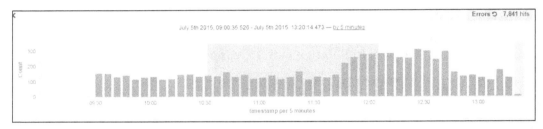

Zoom-in to Set Time Filter

Querying and searching data

Kibana uses Lucene query syntax to search among indices stored in index patterns. You can also specify an Elasticsearch query DSL, like we explained in *Chapter 5, Why Do We Need Elasticsearch in ELK?* The field list, index documents lists, and the histogram are automatically refreshed based on the search and time filter settings.

Analyzed and Not Analyzed Fields

As mentioned in the Logstash index template for Elasticsearch (`https://github.com/logstash-plugins/logstash-output-elasticsearch/blob/master/lib/logstash/outputs/elasticsearch/elasticsearch-template.json`), when we index string fields, both analyzed (tokenized) and non-analyzed versions are saved in indexes. All non-analyzed fields appear with the `.raw` extension in the **Discover** or **Visualize** pages.

Let's look at some examples of searches.

Freetext search

The freetext search is aimed at filtering documents containing the search term. It searches in all the documents for all the fields containing the searched term.

Let's take the following instance as an example:

You want to search for all the ELK books from an index pattern consisting of PacktPub books collections. You can write `'ELK'` in the search box, and it filters all documents containing the term `ELK`.

 Search syntax can be looked up here:
`https://lucene.apache.org/core/2_9_4/ queryparsersyntax.html`

Boolean searches can be performed on the following terms:

AND

`"Learning" AND "ELK"`

The preceding query will search for all documents that contain both terms: `"Learning"` and `"ELK"`.

OR

`"Logstash" OR "ELK`

The preceding query will search for all documents that contain the terms `"Logstash"` or `"ELK"`.

NOT

`"Logstash" NOT "ELK"`

The preceding query will search for documents that contain the term `Logstash` but not `"ELK"`.

Groupings

`("Logstash" OR "ELK")  AND "Kibana"`

The preceding query will search for documents that contain `"Kibana"` and can contain either `"ELK"` or `"Logstash"`.

Wildcard searches

You can also perform wildcard searches using the following terms:

- `plan*`: will search for all documents that have terms, such as `plans`, or `plant`, or `planting`, and so on

- `plan?`: will search for `plant` or `plans`

- `?` and `*`: cannot be used as the first character in a search

Field searches

Field searches aim to search for specific values or ranges of values for fields in your indexed document that displays on the left-hand side of the **Discover** page.

Field searches can be performed using the field name and the `:` character, followed by a value for the field we want to filter on.

```
<field_name>: <field_value>
```

Let's take a look at some examples of field searches:

```
title : "Learning ELK"
title : "Learning ELK" AND  category : "technology"
```

Range searches

Range searches are used to search for a range of values for a field.

For example, to search for a specific date range:

```
date_of_record : [20140701 TO 20141231]
```

To search for a range of values for the `volume` field:

```
volume : [ 100000 TO 200000]
```

Range and field searches can be combined using boolean operators like this:

```
publish_date : [20150701 TO 20151231] AND title : "Learning ELK"
```

Special characters escaping

The following is the list of special characters, which if we want to search for, need to be escaped using the `\` operator:

```
+ - && || ! ( ) { } [ ] ^ " ~ * ? : \
```

For example, to search for `1:2` it needs to be escaped as `1\:2`.

New search

You can start a new search by clicking on the **New Search** button on the
Discover toolbar:

Kibana New Search option

Saving the search

Searches can be saved and used in visualizations later using the **Save Search**
option on the **Discover** toolbar. Saved searches can also be added to a dashboard
in order to show the information in a traditional table format. This is very important
for real-world applications in identifying issues:

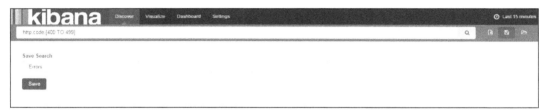

Kibana Save Search option

Loading a search

Previously saved searches can be loaded using the **Load Saved Search** option on the
Discover toolbar:

Loading a Saved Search

Field searches using field list

Field searches can also be performed by clicking on the *positive* or *negative* filter icon on certain values on the field.

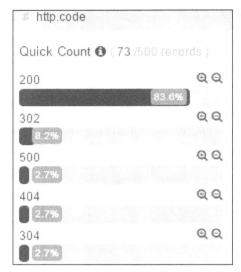

Positive and negative filter on fields using field list

In the preceding figure, if you click on the *positive filter* icon, it will filter all documents having the `http.code` value as `200`, and if you click on *negative filter*, it will show all documents having the `http.code` value other than `200`.

You can also add certain fields on the right-hand side panel by clicking on the *add* button on the field name in the field list. This enables an easy view of fields as tables based on your searches.

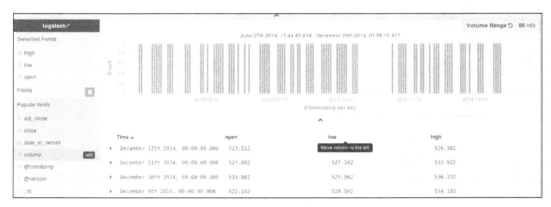

Field Searches in Kibana

In this way, fields can be quickly added and documents can be sorted in fields, and fields can be arranged in any order. This is especially helpful to build a table for a quick search.

Summary

In this chapter, we saw how we can use Kibana's **Discover** page to gain insights into the data with some quick searches, which can be saved and used later.

In the next chapter, we will see the **Visualize**, **Dashboard**, and **Settings** pages in Kibana in detail.

7
Kibana – Visualization and Dashboard

In the last chapter, we looked at the **Discover** page and how we could make some quick searches across indexed documents. In this chapter, we will look at the **Visualize** and **Dashboard** features in Kibana. We will see how we can leverage the power of Kibana, built over Elasticsearch indexes, to build various types of charts and graphs, and awesome dashboards covering various analytics, which can be easily embedded or shared with others.

Visualize page

The **Visualize** page helps create visualizations in the form of graphs and charts. These visualizations can be saved and viewed individually or can be used in multiple dashboards, which act as a collection of visualizations.

All visualizations in Kibana are based on the aggregation feature of Elasticsearch. Kibana also supports multilevel aggregations to come up with various useful data analytics. Let's take a look at what a **Visualize** page looks like:

Kibana Visualize page

The **Visualize** page has two parts—either you can create a new visualization or open an existing one from your saved list.

Creating a visualization

To create a new visualization, select **Visualize** from the top menu bar, which opens a new **Visualize** page, and then click on the **New Visualization** button on tool bar.

Creating a new visualization is a three step process on the **Visualize** page:

1. Select a visualization type.
2. Select a data source (from a new search or an existing saved search).
3. Configure the aggregations (metrics and buckets) that are to be used for the visualization on the **Edit** page.

Visualization types

Kibana supports the following visualizations:

- **Area chart**
- **Data table**
- **Line chart**
- **Markdown widget**
- **Metric**
- **Pie chart**
- **Tile map**
- **Vertical bar chart**

Before we start building visualizations of various types, let's understand a bit about Elasticsearch aggregations, which forms the backbone of the visualizations in Kibana.

Metrics and buckets aggregations

The metrics and buckets concepts come from the aggregation functionality of Elasticsearch, and they play a vital role when designing a visualization for your dataset in Kibana.

Buckets

Buckets help distribute documents among multiple buckets containing a subset of indexed documents. Buckets are very similar to the GROUP BY functionality in SQL. They help group documents based on specified criteria, and metrics can be applied on these documents.

Buckets usually represent the **X-axis** in Kibana charts and it is possible to add sub-buckets to a bucket.

The following buckets are available for the **X-axis** in Kibana:

- **Date Histogram**
- **Histogram**
- **Range**
- **Date Range**

- **IPV4 Range**
- **Terms**
- **Filters**
- **Significant Terms**

Let's take a look at a few important visualizations here.

Date Histogram

Date Histogram requires a field name of type date and interval for the configuration. It groups documents as per the specified field and interval specified. For example, if you specify the field **bucket** as **@timestamp** and **Interval** as **weekly**, documents will be grouped based on weekly data, and then you can apply some metrics, such as **Count**, **Average**, and so on, on top of the grouped documents.

Histogram

Histogram is similar to **Date Histogram**, except that it requires the field of type numbers and a numeric interval to be specified. It will bucket documents for the particular interval specified in the chosen field. This is like a range aggregation with equal intervals.

Range

Range is like **Histogram**, but it allows you to configure different ranges as per the requirements, manually. For example, for a field count, you can choose the bucketing range to be 0-1000, 1000-5000, 5000-15000, and so on.

Date Range

Date Range requires a date field and a custom range to be specified for each bucket.

Terms

Terms help group documents by the value of any field, which is very similar to the GROUP BY statement in SQL. The **Terms** aggregation also lets you choose whether you want **Top N** or **Bottom N**, or you can specify the order based on metrics too. For example, you can choose to group by a product type and get the top five spends in that product type.

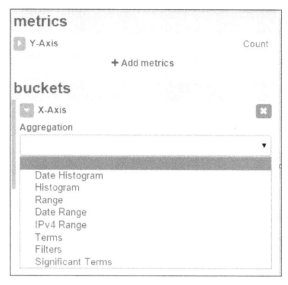

Buckets in visualizations

Metrics

Metrics represents computations performed on values of fields in each bucket, for example, computing the count, average, minimum, or maximum of a field in the document. Metrics usually represent the **Y-axis** in **Area chart**, **Vertical bar chart**, and **Line chart**. The types of metrics available in Kibana are:

- **Count**
- **Average**
- **Sum**
- **Unique Count**
- **Min**
- **Max**
- **Percentile**
- **Percentile Ranks**

Let's take a look at a few of them.

Count

The **Count** metric aggregation is very important, and its main purpose is to calculate the count of the number of fields in each bucket in a bucket aggregation.

For example, to count the number of visitors for each of the product categories, you can specify the product category field as bucket aggregation and count metric aggregation.

Average, Sum, Min, and Max

Similar to **Count** aggregation, **Average**, **Sum**, **Min**, and **Max** provide the average, sum, minimum, and maximum, respectively, of all the values of a numeric field provided in the aggregation.

Unique Count

Unique Count is similar to the COUNT (DISTINCT fieldname) functionality in SQL, which counts number of unique values for a field.

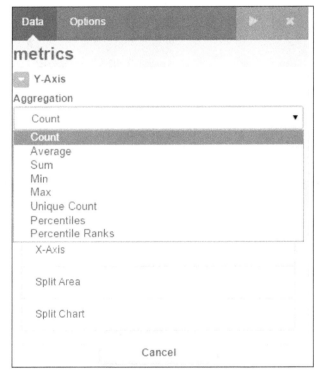

Kibana visualization metrics

Advanced options

Buckets and metrics aggregations have **Advanced** options, which can take JSON input as scripted fields, as described in *Chapter 6, Finding Insights with Kibana*. The following script is an example:

```
{ "script" : "doc['volume'].value * 100"}
```

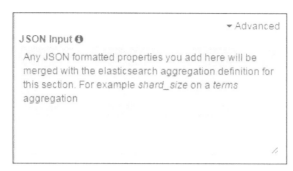

JSON Input Advanced option

Overall, a **New Visualization** page looks like this, with the toolbar at the top, **metrics** and **buckets** configuration on the left and the preview pane on right-hand side:

Kibana New Visualization page

The toolbar at the top has the options to create a new visualization, save a visualization, open a saved visualization, share a visualization, and refresh it.

Kibana Visualization toolbar

When creating a visualization, Kibana provides two options as a search source:

- **From a saved search**
- **From a new search**

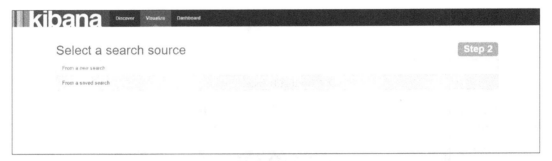

Kibana search source selection

From a saved search uses searches that you saved in the **Discover** page.

From a new search is used to create a new visualization based on a new search.

Visualizations

Now, let's take a look at various visualization types and how they can be used.

Area chart

Area chart is especially useful to create stacked timelines or distribute data.

Area chart uses **metrics** as **Y-axis** and **buckets** for **X-axis**. We can also define sub-aggregations in **buckets**, which give you the functionality of **Split Charts** (multiple charts based on different aggregations) or **Split Area** (Area chart split based on different aggregations).

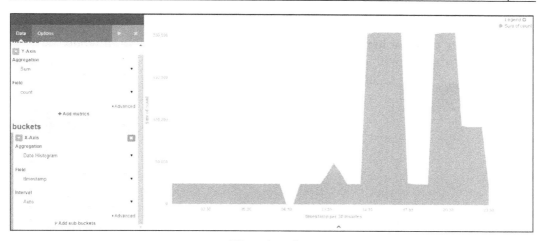

Kibana Area chart

Data table

Data table is used to present aggregated data in a tabular format and helps identify **Top N** kinds of aggregations.

For example, to get the top five clients by the number of hits, the following data table visualization can be used:

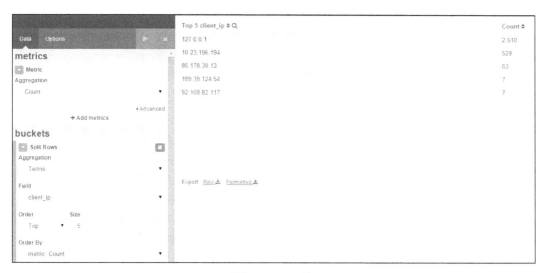

Kibana Data table

Line chart

Line charts are used for high density time series, and are often helpful when comparing one series with another:

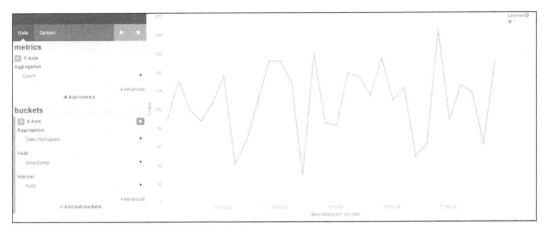

Kibana Line chart

Markdown widget

Markdown widget is used to display information or instructions on **Dashboard** and can be used for any requirements for text on **Dashboard**.

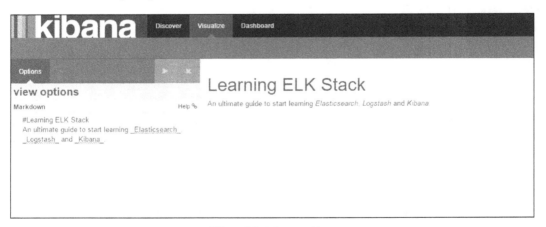

Kibana Markdown widget

Metric

Metric is used to show a one number kind of analysis for your field. It can be used to compute the total number of hits or the sum or average of a field.

For example, the following metric can be used to show the average response time of the application over a period of time:

Kibana Metric

Pie chart

Pie charts are often used to show parts of a whole or a percentage relationship. It represents the distribution of data over multiple slices in a pie chart.

A slice of the pie chart is determined by metrics aggregations, which can have the values **Count**, **Sum**, or **Unique Count**. Bucket aggregation defines the type of data that has to be represented in one chart.

For example, the following pie chart can be used to show the distribution of the different response codes of an application:

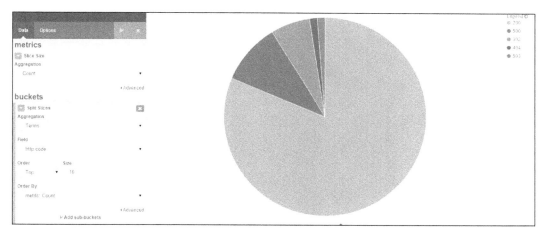

Kibana Pie chart

Tile map

Tile maps are used to locate geographic locations based on geo coordinates. It works on the **Geohash** bucket aggregation, which groups multiple coordinates into one bucket.

Kibana Tile map

Vertical bar chart

Vertical bar chart is a chart that can be used for a variety of purposes and works well with time- and non-time-based fields. It can be used as single bar or stacked as well.

Y-axis is **metrics** and **X-axis** is **buckets** aggregation.

For example, the following Vertical bar chart can be used to show a count of HTTP response codes:

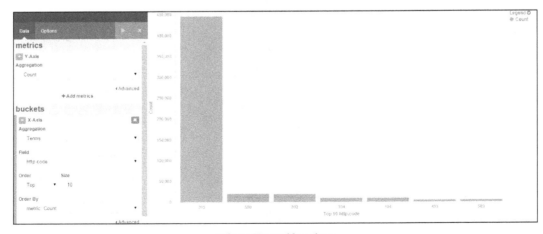

Kibana Vertical bar chart

Dashboard page

Kibana **Dashboard** is just a collection of saved visualizations or saved searches, which can be arranged in any order. Visualizations can be used on multiple dashboards and changes will reflect to all of them automatically. A dashboard can be saved and shared easily.

Let's look at what **Dashboard** will look like:

Building a new dashboard

When you click on the Kibana **Dashboard** page link at the top of the page for the first time, it displays an empty Kibana dashboard that is ready to add visualizations to:

Kibana New Dashboard screen

You can click on the **+** button with a circle on the extreme right-hand side toolbar to add any saved visualizations or searches that you saved in the **Discover** page in a tabular format. After you have added the visualizations, you can move the individual visualizations around, edit them, or remove them. You can even resize or drag and drop them as per your requirements.

Setting a refresh interval on the time filter at the top automatically refreshes the dashboard with the latest values.

The *click to filter* feature in Kibana dashboards is very useful in scenarios where you would like all visualizations and searches to reflect events at a particular time. For example, you can click on a specific bar in a histogram and all the other visualizations and searches will reflect the same automatically.

Saving and loading a dashboard

Once you are done with the arrangement of visualizations, to save a dashboard, click on the **Save Dashboard** button on the toolbar and enter a name for the dashboard and save.

Kibana provides the facility to save a dashboard, which reflects values at a particular time. To do this, there is an option to save time with the dashboard. This is useful to provide snapshots of the system at a particular time.

Kibana Save Dashboard

To load a saved dashboard, click on the **Load Dashboard** button on the toolbar and choose among a list of saved dashboards.

Sharing a dashboard

Once completed and saved, you can share a link to a dashboard or embed it within another application using the IFrame tag. To do so, click on the **Share** button on the toolbar, which shows both a code to embed within another application, and a direct link to the dashboard, which can be copied and shared.

Kibana Share screen

Summary

In this chapter, we've seen how to create different types of visualizations in Kibana based on aggregations. We also saw how to arrange and share them using Kibana **Dashboards**. In the next chapter, we'll see how we can put all the components of ELK together to build a powerful data pipeline.

8
Putting It All Together

In the previous chapters, we looked at the basics of Elasticsearch, Kibana, and Logstash. We saw the configurations and properties of each of them, and tried to understand what role each of the components plays in building a data pipeline for your data.

Now we will apply everything that we have learnt so far. We'll create an end-to-end running solution to analyze logs using ELK Stack.

For demo purposes, we will use a sample web application that runs on the Tomcat server. We'll set up ELK Stack, where we'll use Logstash to collect, parse and index access logs to Elasticsearch. Finally, we'll see various searches and visualizations on it in the Kibana interface.

Input dataset

The input dataset is a continuous stream of Tomcat access logs in the following format:

```
10.0.0.2 - - [08/Sep/2015:17:39:46 +0100] "GET /elk/demo/10 HTTP/1.1" 200
40
10.0.0.2 - - [08/Sep/2015:17:39:47 +0100] "GET /elk/demo/11 HTTP/1.1" 200
39
10.0.0.3 - - [08/Sep/2015:17:39:48 +0100] "GET /elk/demo/12 HTTP/1.1" 200
39
10.0.0.2 - - [08/Sep/2015:17:39:49 +0100] "GET /elk/demo/13 HTTP/1.1" 200
39
10.0.0.2 - - [08/Sep/2015:17:39:50 +0100] "GET /elk/demo/14 HTTP/1.1" 200
39
10.0.0.4 - - [08/Sep/2015:17:39:51 +0100] "GET /elk/demo/15 HTTP/1.1" 200
40
10.0.0.2 - - [08/Sep/2015:17:39:52 +0100] "GET /elk/demo/16 HTTP/1.1" 200
39
```

```
10.0.0.2 - - [08/Sep/2015:17:39:53 +0100] "GET /elk/demo/17 HTTP/1.1" 200
39
10.0.0.5 - - [08/Sep/2015:17:39:54 +0100] "GET /elk/demo/18 HTTP/1.1" 200
39
10.0.0.2 - - [08/Sep/2015:17:39:55 +0100] "GET /elk/demo/19 HTTP/1.1" 200
39
10.0.0.2 - - [08/Sep/2015:17:39:56 +0100] "GET /elk/demo/20 HTTP/1.1" 200
40
10.0.0.6 - - [08/Sep/2015:17:39:57 +0100] "GET /elk/demo/21 HTTP/1.1" 200
38
10.0.0.2 - - [08/Sep/2015:17:39:58 +0100] "GET /elk/demo/22 HTTP/1.1" 200
40
10.0.0.2 - - [08/Sep/2015:17:39:59 +0100] "GET /elk/demo/23 HTTP/1.1" 200
39
```

The preceding log format is a Common Apache log format, defined in the Tomcat `server.xml` file in `conf` folder as follows:

```
<Valve className="org.apache.catalina.valves.AccessLogValve"
directory="logs"
              prefix="localhost_access_log." suffix=".txt"
              pattern="%h %l %u %t &quot;%r&quot; %s %b" />
```

The log pattern is in the following format:

```
%h %l %u %t "%r" %s %b
```

- `%h`: This represents the remote hostname (or IP address)
- `%l`: This represents the remote logical username
- `%u`: This represents the remote user that was authenticated
- `%t`: This specifies the date and time in common log format
- `%r`: This represents the request
- `%s`: This represents the response HTTP code
- `%b`: This represents the bytes sent in response, excluding HTTP headers

Configuring Logstash input

In this section, we'll configure Logstash to read data from access logs located on Tomcat, and index it in Elasticsearch, making filters and tokenization of terms in logs as per the grok pattern.

Grok pattern for access logs

As we already saw, some of the commonly used grok patterns are already included with the Logstash installation. Check out the list of Logstash grok patterns on GitHub at `https://github.com/logstash-plugins/logstash-patterns-core/tree/master/patterns`.

There is already a grok pattern for the Common Apache log format in the Logstash installation as follows:

```
COMMONAPACHELOG %{IPORHOST:clientip} %{USER:ident} %{USER:auth}
\[%{HTTPDATE:timestamp}\] "(?:%{WORD:verb} %{NOTSPACE:request}(?:
HTTP/%{NUMBER:httpversion})?|%{DATA:rawrequest})"
%{NUMBER:response} (?:%{NUMBER:bytes}|-)
```

We can directly use COMMONAPACHELOG as a matching pattern for our incoming messages to Logstash as follows:

```
input{
file{
path =>"/var/lib/tomcat7/logs/localhost_access_logs.txt"
start_position =>"beginning"
}
}
```

Next, we need to specify our grok pattern matching with the incoming message, assign a timestamp field from our message, and convert the data types of some of the fields as per our needs:

```
filter{
 grok {
      match => { "message" => "%{COMMONAPACHELOG}" }
    }

date{
    match => ["timestamp","dd/MMM/yyyy:HH:mm:ss Z"]
}
mutate{
convert => ["response","integer"]
convert => ["bytes","integer"]
}
}
```

Finally, to configure the output plugin to send filtered messages to Elasticsearch, we will not specify any port here as we are using the default port for Elasticsearch, that is, 9200:

```
output{
elasticsearch {
host => "localhost"
}
}
```

Now that we have understood the individual configuration, let's see what the overall configuration for Tomcat looks like:

```
input{
file{
path =>"/var/lib/tomcat7/logs/localhost_access_log.txt"
start_position =>"beginning"
}
}

filter{
 grok {
      match => { "message" => "%{COMMONAPACHELOG}" }
    }

date{
    match => ["timestamp","dd/MMM/yyyy:HH:mm:ss Z"]
}
mutate{
convert => ["response","integer"]
convert => ["bytes","integer"]
}
}
output{
elasticsearch {
host => "localhost"
}
}
```

*

Now, lets start logstash with this configuration:

$ bin/logstash -f logstash.conf

Logstash will start to run with the defined configuration and keep on indexing all incoming events to the Elasticsearch indexes. You may see an output that is similar to this one on the console:

```
May 31, 2015 4:04:54 PM org.elasticsearch.node.internal.InternalNode
start
INFO: [logstash-4004-9716] started
Logstash startup completed
```

Now, you will see your Apache access logs data in Elasticsearch. Logstash was able to parse the input line and break it into different pieces of information, based on the grok patterns, for the Apache access logs. Now, we can easily set up analytics on HTTP response codes, request methods, and different URLs.

At this point, we can open the Elasticsearch Kopf plugin console that we installed in *Chapter 1, Introduction to ELK Stack*, to verify whether we have some documents indexed already, and we can also query these documents.

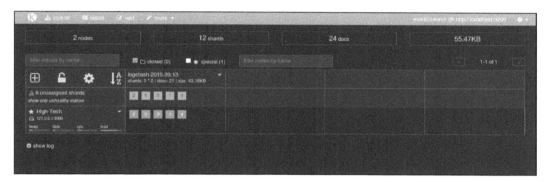

Elasticsearch Kopf UI

If we can see some indexes for Logstash already in Elasticsearch, we have verified that our Logstash configuration worked well.

Visualizing with Kibana

Now that you have verified that your data is indexed successfully in Elasticsearch, we can go ahead and look at the Kibana interface to get some useful analytics from the data.

Running Kibana

As described in *Chapter 1, Introduction to ELK Stack*, we will start the Kibana service from the Kibana installation directory:

```
$ bin/kibana
```

Now, let's see Kibana up and running with a screen similar to the following screenshot on the browser with this URL:

```
http://localhost:5601
```

We can verify our index and fields in the **Settings** page under the indices tab as follows:

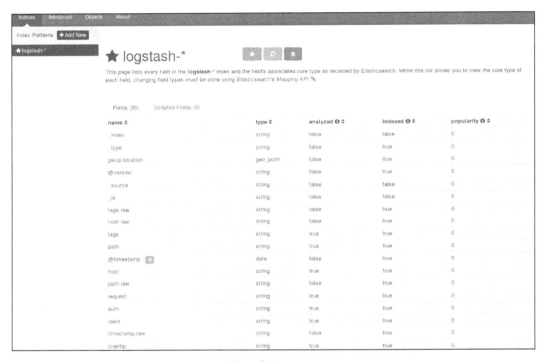

Kibana Settings page

It shows all our fields that were indexed, their data types, index status, and popularity value.

As we have already set up Kibana to take the `logstash-*` indexes by default, it starts to display the indexed data as a histogram of counts, and the associated data as fields in the JSON format as follows:

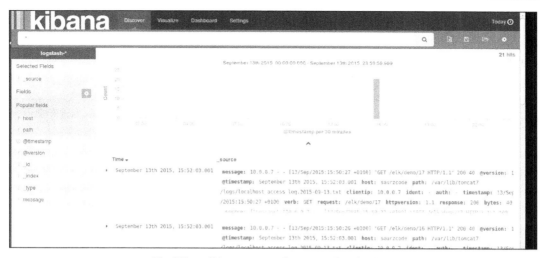

The Kibana Discover page showing indexed values

Searching on the Discover page

After our data is indexed, we can perform some quick searches on our fields to analyze some data.

To search for a specific client IP, we can type search command as `clientip: 10.0.0.7` and the indexed document on the page displays matching highlighted values:

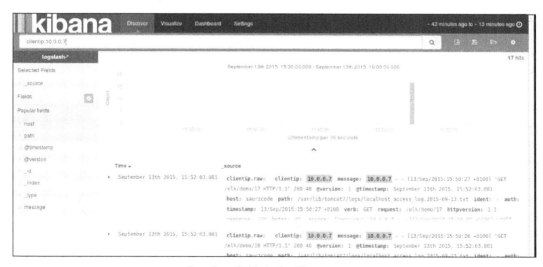

Search on fields in the Discover page

To search all GET requests coming from specific client IP, we can issue a query like this:

```
clientip:10.0.0.7 AND  verb:GET
```

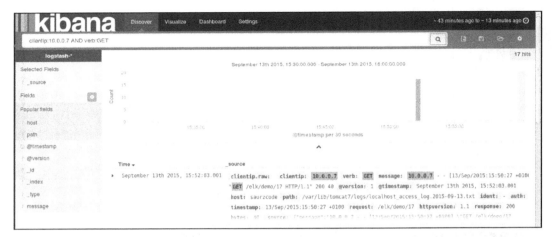

Searching on fields

To search all instances of a particular GET request coming from a specific client IP we can issue a query like the one shown in the following screenshot:

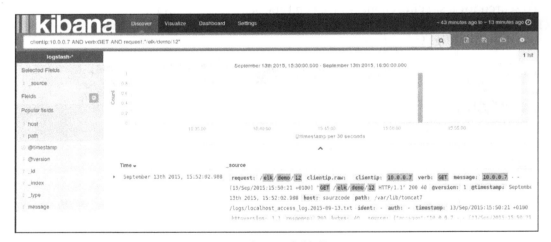

Searching on fields II

Once our data is fully indexed, the **Discover** page will look something like this, with a default histogram based on the count of documents over time:

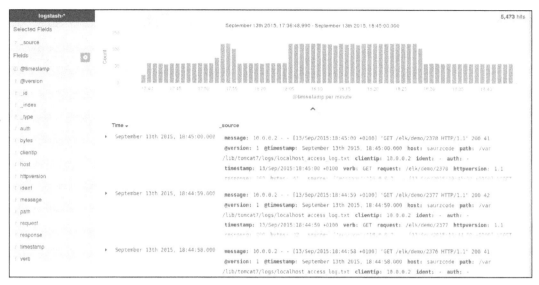

The Discover page after full indexing

Visualizations – charts

Let's build some basic visualizations from the Kibana **Visualize** page, and we will use them later in dashboard.

Click on the **Visualize** page link at the top of the Kibana home page and click on the new visualization icon.

This page shows various types of visualizations that are possible with the
Kibana interface:

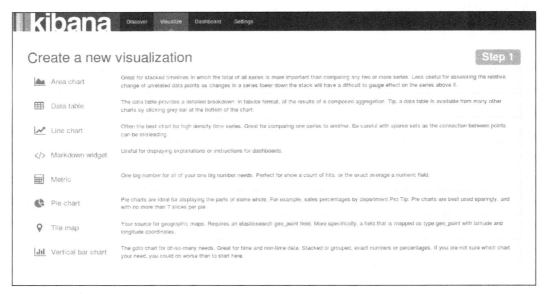

Kibana visualization menu

Building a Line chart

The first visualization that we will build is a **Line chart** showing the number of hits over time for the application. To do this, we'll choose the **Y-axis metrics** as **Count** and the **X-axis bucket** as **Date Histogram**, and then click on **Apply**. The resulting **Line chart** looks like this:

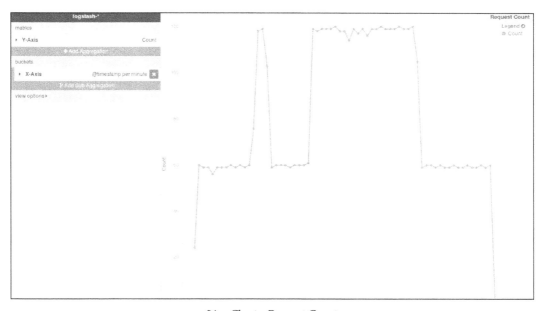

Line Chart – Request Count

Now, save the visualization using any name for the **Line chart**, which we will pull in **Dashboard** later.

Building an Area chart

We can build an **Area chart** based on the number of bytes transferred over time as follows. To do this, we'll choose the **Y-axis metrics** as **Average** and choose **Field** as **bytes**. The resulting **Area chart** looks like this:

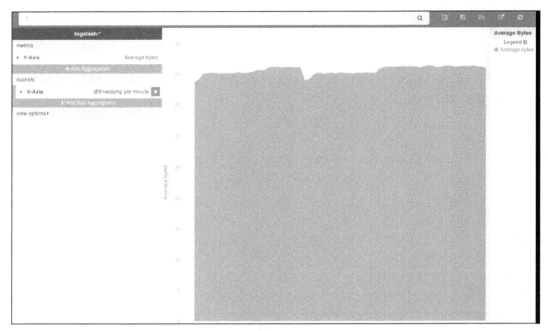

Area Chart – Average Bytes

Now, save the visualization using any name for the **Area chart**, which we will pull in **Dashboard** later.

Building a Bar chart

We'll build a vertical split bar chart showing the number of requests split across multiple clients. For the **Y-axis metrics**, we will use **Count**, and for the **X-axis aggregation**, we'll use **Date Histogram**. We'll use sub aggregation using the **Split Bars** feature, and split it using the **clientip** term:

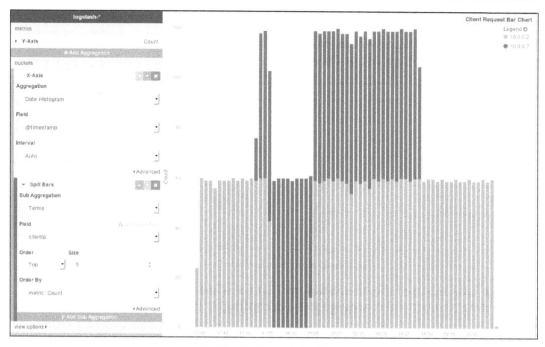

Bar Chart – Requests by Clients

Now, save the visualization using any name for the **Bar chart**, which we will pull in **Dashboard** later.

Building a Markdown

Markdown is lightweight markup language that has a simple formatting syntax for various documentation needs. We'll build one Markdown to give an explanation of our **Dashboard**:

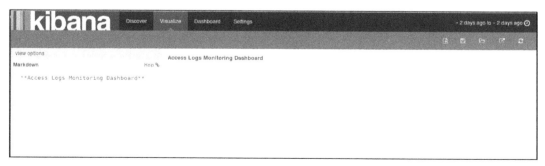

Markdown

Dashboard page

On the **Dashboard** page, we can choose from our list of saved visualizations or searches to include them in our **Dashboard**:

Add visualization or searches to Dashboard

After we have selected the visualizations that we want to include in our dashboard, we can drag and drop and arrange them accordingly. The resulting dashboard looks like this:

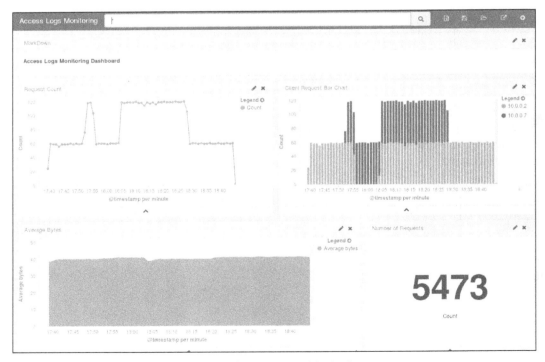

Dashboard – Access Logs Monitoring

Once completed, we can choose to share the dashboard using the share button, which also gives us the code to be used if we want to include it as an embedded dashboard in some other application:

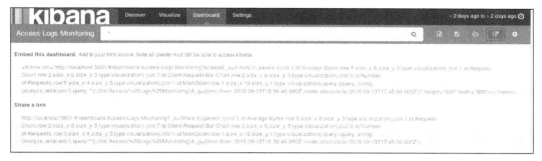

Share Dashboard

Summary

In this chapter, we saw how we could build an end-to-end data pipeline built over our logs using ELK Stack, which helps us get useful analysis from our data. This chapter helped us understand how the features of Elasticsearch, Logstash, and Kibana come together to help build our own analytics pipeline.

In the next chapter, we'll take a look at some of the practical implementations of ELK Stack and how it is helping the industry.

9
ELK Stack in Production

So far in the book, we saw how we could use ELK stack to figure out useful information out of our logs, and build a centralized logging solution for multiple data sources of an application.

In our end-to-end log pipeline, we configured ELK on our local machine to use local Elasticsearch, Logstash, and Kibana instances.

In this chapter, we will take a look at how ELK Stack can be used in production with huge amounts of data and a variety of data sources. Some of the biggest companies, such as Bloomberg, LinkedIn, Netflix, and so on, are successfully using ELK Stack in production and ELK Stack is gaining popularity day by day.

When we talk about the production level implementation of ELK Stack, some of the perquisites are:

- Prevention of data loss
- Data protection
- Scalability of the solution
- Data retention

Prevention of data loss

Data loss prevention is critical for a production system, as monitoring and debugging is largely dependent on each and every log event to be present in the system; otherwise, whole analytics or the debugging system will fail, and we end up losing some of the important events in our system.

Data loss can be prevented using a message broker in front of the Logstash indexers. Message brokers, such as Redis, prove to be useful when dealing with a large stream of data, as Logstash may slow down while indexing data to Elasticsearch. Redis can help in these situations where it can buffer the data while Logstash is busy indexing to Elasticsearch. It also adds a layer of resiliency where if indexing fails, events are held in a queue instead of getting lost. ZeroMQ, RabbitMQ, AMQP can also be used as a broker in place of Redis.

For example, the following architecture can be useful:

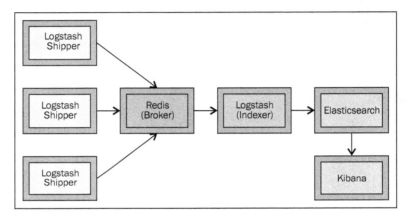

ELK Architecture with message broker

Data protection

Since data is of immense value and carries a lot of confidential information, it is extremely important to protect the data at various points while in ELK Stack. Elasticsearch indices must be prevented from unauthorized access, and Kibana Dashboard should be protected too. We can also set up an Nginx reverse proxy to access Kibana instances, which will put your Kibana console behind an authentication page that requires a username and password.

Kibana supports SSL encryption for both client requests and the requests the Kibana server sends to Elasticsearch.

To encrypt communications between the browser and the Kibana server, we can configure the `ssl_key_file` and `ssl_cert_file` properties in `kibana.yml`:

The following are SSL for outgoing requests from the Kibana server (PEM formatted):

- `ssl_key_file`: /path/to/your/server.key
- `ssl_cert_file`: /path/to/your/server.crt

Elasticsearch shield can be used to provide index level access control to your data in Elasticsearch. We can create a role for Kibana in shield, and determine what access we want to grant to users of Kibana, as follows:

```
kibana4:
  cluster:
      - cluster:monitor/nodes/info
      - cluster:monitor/health
  indices:
    '*':
      - indices:admin/mappings/fields/get
      - indices:admin/validate/query
      - indices:data/read/search
      - indices:data/read/msearch
      - indices:admin/get
    '.kibana':
      - indices:admin/exists
      - indices:admin/mapping/put
      - indices:admin/mappings/fields/get
      - indices:admin/refresh
      - indices:admin/validate/query
      - indices:data/read/get
      - indices:data/read/mget
      - indices:data/read/search
      - indices:data/write/delete
      - indices:data/write/index
      - indices:data/write/update
      - indices:admin/create
```

We can also give the Kibana server level roles, which gives access to the `.kibana` index as follows:

```
kibana4_server:
  cluster:
      - cluster:monitor/nodes/info
      - cluster:monitor/health
  indices:
    '.kibana':
      - indices:admin/create
      - indices:admin/exists
      - indices:admin/mapping/put
      - indices:admin/mappings/fields/get
      - indices:admin/refresh
      - indices:admin/validate/query
      - indices:data/read/get
      - indices:data/read/mget
      - indices:data/read/search
      - indices:data/write/delete
      - indices:data/write/index
      - indices:data/write/update
```

Please note that shield is not free and is a part of a paid service provided by Elastic. Search Guard is another tool that is free and works well to secure your Elasticsearch installation. More details are available at `http://floragunn.com/searchguard`.

System scalability

As the data in the application grows, it is essential that the log analytics system should scale well with the system. Also, there are times when your systems are under a heavy load, and you need your log analytics systems to analyze what is going on with the application. ELK Stack provides that capability where you can easily scale each component as per your needs. You can always add more Elasticsearch nodes (master nodes and data nodes) in the cluster. It is recommended that you have three master nodes (one primary and two backup) for large clusters. Also, load balancing or routing nodes can be added for high volume searches and indexing requirements. You can also get more Logstash and Redis instances, and add more than one Kibana instance too. A typical scaled architecture may look like this:

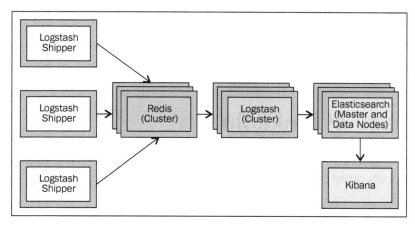

ELK Architecture with Cluster

Data retention

When setting up a log analytics system, it is extremely important to define your data retention policy as Elasticsearch can't hold all the data that you have, which may result in data loss. There should be a process to automatically delete old indices after a certain defined period.

The Elasticsearch Curator (https://github.com/elasticsearch/curator) is especially useful to manage your indices. You can schedule Curator to delete old indices based on your need. For example, the following command can be set up in a crontab to delete indices older than 10 days at a specified time, daily:

```
curator --host 10.0.0.7 delete indices --older-than 10 --time-unit days \
--timestring '%Y.%m.%d'
```

ELK Stack implementations

The ELK community is quite large, and it's growing rapidly as it is gaining more and more attention. Let's take a look at some of the already existing successful ELK Stack implementations.

ELK Stack at LinkedIn

LinkedIn is a business oriented social networking site, which is mainly used for professional networking. LinkedIn was launched in May 5, 2003. As of March 2015, LinkedIn reports more than 364 million acquired users, in more than 200 countries and territories.

Refer to `http://www.slideshare.net/TinLe1/elk-atlinked-in`.

Problem statement

LinkedIn has millions of multiple data centers, tens of thousands of servers, hundreds of billions of log records. It is a challenge to log, index, search, store, visualize, and analyze all of these logs all day, every day. Also, security in terms of access control, storage, and transport has to be maintained. As data grows, the system will scale to more data centers, more servers, and will produce even more logs. It needs an efficient log analytics pipeline that can handle data at this scale.

Criteria for solution

The log analytics solution that LinkedIn is looking for, must meet the following:

- It is horizontally scalable, so that more nodes can be added when needed
- It is fast, and quick, and as close to real-time as possible
- It is inexpensive
- It is flexible
- It has a large user community and supports availability
- It is open source

Solution

ELK Stack proved to match all these criteria. ELK is currently used across many teams in LinkedIn. This is what the current ELK Stack implementation at LinkedIn looks like:

- 100 plus ELK clusters across 20 plus teams and six data centers
- Some of the larger clusters have:
    - Greater than 32 billion docs (30+ TB)
    - Daily indices that average 3.0 billion docs (~3 TB)

The current architecture for ELK Stack at LinkedIn uses Elasticsearch, Logstash, Kibana, and Kafka.

 Apache Kafka: Kafka is a high throughput distributed messaging system, which was invented by LinkedIn, and open sourced in 2011. It is a fast, scalable, distributed, and durable messaging system which proves useful for systems that produce huge amounts of data. More details can be found at the Kafka site `http://kafka.apache.org`.

Kafka at LinkedIn

Kafka is a common data-transport layer across LinkedIn. Kafka handles around 1.1 trillion messages per day, a 200 TB per day input, and a 700 TB per day output. The architecture is spread across 1100 brokers, over 50 plus clusters, which includes around 32000 topics and 350 thousands partitions.

Operational challenges

LinkedIn generates lots of data, so reliable transport, queuing, storing, and indexing is very essential. It has to take data from various sources, such as Java, Scala, Python, Node.js, Go, and so on. Obviously, the data format was different across these sources so transformations were needed.

Logging using Kafka at LinkedIn

LinkedIn uses dedicated clusters for logs in each data center. They have individual Kafka topics per application, and it acts as a common logging transport for all services, languages, and frameworks. To ingest logs from Kafka to Logstash, they used their own Kafka input plugin; later, they started using KCC (Kafka console consumer) using a pipe input plugin.

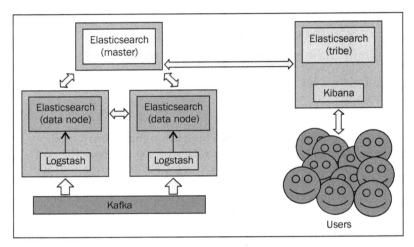

ELK at LinkedIn

An example configuration of a Logstash pipe plugin using KCC is as follows:

```
pipe {
    type => "mobile"
    command => "/opt/bin/kafka-console-consumer/kafka-console-
consumer.sh \
        --formatter
com.linkedin.avro.KafkaMessageJsonWithHexFormatter \
        --property schema.registry.url=http://schema-
server.example.com:12250/schemaRegistry/schemas \
        --autocommit.interval.ms=60000 \
        --zookeeper zk.example.com:12913/kafka-metrics \
        --topic log_stash_event \
        --group logstash1"
    codec => "json"
}
```

ELK at SCA

SCA is a leading global hygiene and forest products company. The SCA group companies develop and produce sustainable personal care, tissue, and forest products. As we can see at `https://www.elastic.co/blog/improving-user-intelligence-with-the-elk-stack-at-sca`:

> *"At SCA we use Elasticsearch, Logstash, and Kibana to record searches, clicks on result documents and user feedback, on both the intranet and external sites. We also collect qualitative metrics by asking our public users a question after showing search results: "Did you find what you were looking for?" The user has the option to give a thumbs up or down and also write a comment."*

How is ELK used in SCA?

All search parameters and results information are recorded for each search event: the query string, paging, sorting, facets, the number of hits, search response time, the date and time of the search, and so on. Clicking a result document also records a multitude of information: the position of the document in the result list, the time it took from search to click, and various document metadata (such as URL, source, format, last modified, author, and more). A click event also gets connected with the search event that generated it. This is also the case for feedback events.

Each event is written to a log file that is being monitored by Logstash, which then creates a document from each event, and pushes them to Elasticsearch where the data is visualized in Kibana.

How is it helping in analytics?

Since a lot of information is being indexed in the stack, a variety of analytics can be performed from simple queries, such as "What are the ten most frequent queries during the past week?" and "Users who click on document X, what do they search for?", to the more complex ones, such as "What is the distribution of clicked documents' last modified dates, coming from source S, on Wednesdays?"

Analysis like this helps them tune the search to meet the needs of the users and deliver value to them. It helps adjust the relevance model, add new facets or remove old ones, or change the layout of search and result pages.

What this means for SCA is that they get a search that is ever improving. The direct feedback loop between the users and administrators of the system creates a sense of community, especially when users see that their grievances are being tended to. Users find what they are looking for to a greater and greater extent, saving them time and frustration.

ELK for monitoring at SCA

This setup is not only used to record information about user behavior, but also used to monitor the health of the servers. In that context Elasticsearch, Logstash, and Kibana are being used as a *Time Series Database*. Every few seconds, information about each server's CPU, memory, and disk usage (time series data) is being indexed. It also helps gain access to the historic aspect of data and to find trends in the system. This can, of course, be correlated with the user statistics. For example, a rise in CPU usage can be correlated to an increase in query volume.

Refer to: `https://www.elastic.co/blog/improving-user-intelligence-with-the-elk-stack-at-sca`.

ELK at Cliffhanger Solutions

Cliffhanger Solutions is an application and service provider for the utility and telecom industry. It helps customers and utility companies with preventative maintenance and reducing outage restoration times.

> *"At Cliffhanger Solutions, we index data in real time from various sources using Elasticsearch and Logstash. Sources include GPS location data from maintenance trucks or from tablets running our app, readings from smart meters and facility data from* **GIS (geographical information systems)***."*

Kibana dashboard at Cliffhanger

Operators can now quickly get answers to questions such as "Can I safely close this switch and restore power to these 1500 customers?" or "A storm is coming in from the South, how fast can I get my bucket trucks to the area where the storm will hit?" As for preventative maintenance, engineers can seek answers to questions such as "Transformers from vendor X have a higher than average **MTBF (mean time between failures)**. Find all of them and sort them by installation date, then send them to the work order system for inspection or replacement." While it might not sound like a big deal, this is actually pretty incredible, and this wasn't possible until now without a heavy investments in consultancy or getting locked in with the few *one stop shop* large vendors that offer a total solution. As we can see at `https://www.elastic.co/blog/using-elk-to-keep-the-lights-on`:

"Cliffhanger Solutions is a small company, but the flexibility of Elasticsearch allowed us to focus on creating value for our customers instead of getting stuck in maintaining different systems for different clients. And our clients are getting it as well. For example, we serve a tiny utility on a Caribbean island, with only 1 guy in the IT department. By using ATLAS (+Kibana) out of the box, we built them a dashboard to show them outages on a map, color coded by customer density. This would never have been possible even a few years ago. The ELK stack is pretty incredible at making data searchable even if the source data is not clearly defined. Unlike traditional databases you don't need to know your questions in advance, you can explore and find correlations you didn't even know existed. It reduces a lot of overhead.

Internally, at the Cliffhanger office, we use the ELK stack to monitor the status of our clients' applications. We use it to improve search relevance, performance, find errors and prevent hack attacks. We share this data with our clients. They like this level of transparency and it gives them confidence that their data is safe."

Refer to `https://www.elastic.co/blog/using-elk-to-keep-the-lights-on`.

Kibana demo – Packetbeat dashboard

Finally, from ELK itself, there is a very good demo for the Kibana dashboard, which shows various aspects of the stack, and shows the power and breadth of information it gives. It is available at `http://demo.elastic.co`.

 Packetbeat is a real-time network packet analytics provider, and an open source data shipper that integrates with Elasticsearch and Kibana to provide real-time analytics for web, database, and other network protocols.

This demo is spread across multiple dashboards based on Packetbeat, such as the MySQL dashboard, the MongoDB dashboard, the Web Transactions dashboard, the Thrift-RPC and PostgreSQL dashboard. It helps us understand many advanced searches and visualizations built on the Kibana platform. Here is what the dashboard looks like:

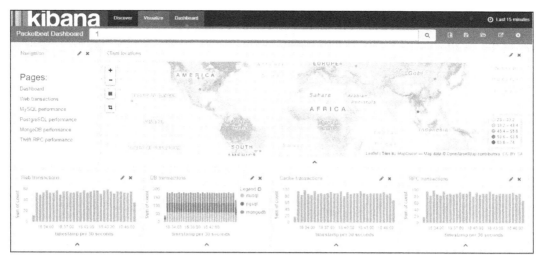

Kibana Packetbeat Demo dashboard

As we can see on the left-hand side of the preceding screenshot, it displays links to various dashboards. A MySQL performance dashboard, which displays the various queries used, performance of queries, and so on, looks like this:

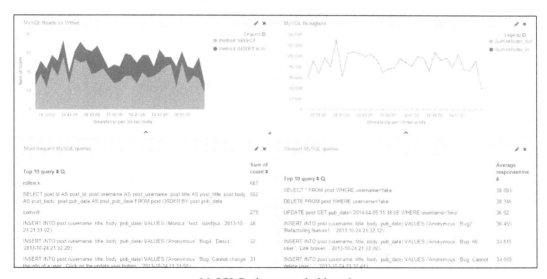

MySQL Performance dashboard

A Web Transactions dashboard, which displays various web transactions, which includes the various HTTP methods used, total number of requests, error codes, and so on, looks like this:

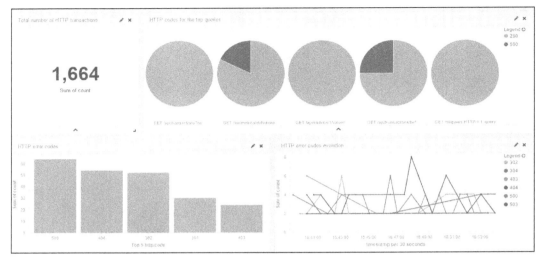

Web Transactions dashboard

A MongoDB dashboard, which dispays MongoDB throughput, errors, errors per collections, input and output throughput, and so on, looks like this:

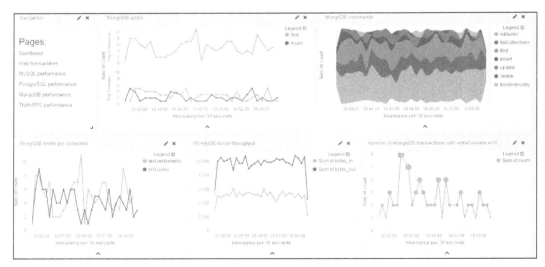

MongoDB Performance dashboard

We can also explore multiple visualizations built in each of these dashboards. For example, a configuration of a GeoIP visualization, which plots clients across the geography, looks like this:

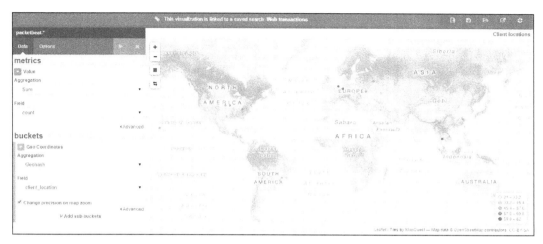

Geo IP Visualization

Summary

In this chapter, we looked at some of the production level strategies for ELK Stack and also looked at some of the implementations of the stack. ELK Stack is gaining more popularity as the community of users evolves, and with a multitude of use cases, which get benefits from the stack.

10
Expanding Horizons with ELK

In all the previous chapters, we explored all the capabilities of ELK Stack, and how it makes your life easier to analyze logs. Now, we will explore some of the plugins and utilities that extend the capability of the stack and make it more wonderful, secure, and easy to maintain. We'll also take a look at the roadmap for the components of ELK Stack.

The following topics are covered in this chapter:

- Elasticsearch plugins and utilities
  - Curator for index management
  - Shield for security
  - Marvel to monitor

- ELK roadmap

Elasticsearch plugins and utilities

Elasticsearch is a very important component of ELK Stack, so it's very important to have a good management of the Elasticsearch cluster, and to maintain security. There are a few plugins and utilities that are available.

Curator for index management

Curator is an important utility that helps manage the Elasticsearch indices. As your data grows, it becomes important to manage the kind of information that you want to retain and what information you can remove from your system. Curator can help remove old indices and optimize the system.

The following are some of the high level tasks that Curator can perform for your Elasticsearch indices:

- Delete indices and snapshots
- Close indices
- Open closed indices
- Show indices and snapshots
- Add or remove indices from an alias
- Optimize indices
- Change the number of replicas per shard for indices

Curator commands

Curator can be easily configured as cron entries in your system, where you can schedule the cleanup of indices regularly. Let's take a look at the command-line syntax of Curator:

```
curator [FLAGS] COMMAND [FLAGS] SUBCOMMAND [FLAGS]
```

All available options can be explored using the `help` command:

```
curator --help
```

Let's look at some examples of how Curator can be used:

- Deleting the indices older than a certain period:
  ```
  curator --host 10.0.0.X delete indices --older-than 180 --time-unit days \ --timestring '%Y.%m.%d'
  ```

- Show all the indices matching a timestring:
  ```
  curator --host 10.0.0.x show indices --timestring '%Y.%m.%d'
  ```

- Add indices older than 30 days to `alias last_month`:
  ```
  curator alias --alias-older-than 30 --alias last_month
  ```

- Remove indices older than `60` days from `alias last_month`:
  ```
  curator alias --unalias-older-than 60 --alias last_month
  ```

Curator installation

Curator installation is very easy and quick; it can be done via the python pip utility:

```
pip install elasticsearch-curator
```

Curator is hosted at `https://github.com/elastic/curator`, and detailed information about Curator can be found in its official documentation at `https://www.elastic.co/guide/en/elasticsearch/client/curator/current/index.html`.

Shield for security

Shield is an Elasticsearch plugin from Elastic that adds security to your Elasticsearch cluster. Shield helps protect the data by adding a secure authentication or role-based authorization process.

The following are high-level capabilities of shield:

- It adds authorization control to cluster by enabling password protection, role-based access control, and IP filtering techniques
- It adds SSL/TLS encryption, and message authentication capability
- It adds auditing capabilities to maintain an audit trail of changes in data

> More details on shield can be found in its official documentation here:
>
> `https://www.elastic.co/guide/en/shield/current/index.html`

Shield is available for 30 days with a trial license, and a subscription needs to be purchased after that. There are open sources alternatives for shield for Elasticsearch security, such as Search Guard (`https://github.com/floragunncom/search-guard`).

Shield installation

To install shield, you need to follow these steps from the Elasticsearch installation directory:

1. Install the license plugin:

   ```
   bin/plugin -i elasticsearch/license/latest

   -> Installing elasticsearch/license/latest...
   Trying http://download.elasticsearch.org/elasticsearch/license/
   license-latest.zip...
   Downloading ...................................................
   DONE
   Installed elasticsearch/license/latest into /usr/share/
   elasticsearch/plugins/license
   ```

2. Install the shield plugin:

```
bin/plugin -i elasticsearch/shield/latest

-> Installing elasticsearch/shield/latest...
Trying http://download.elasticsearch.org/elasticsearch/shield/
shield-latest.zip...
Downloading
DONE
Installed elasticsearch/shield/latest into /usr/share/
elasticsearch/plugins/shield
```

3. After installing plugin, start your Elasticsearch instance and check in the start up logs for references of shield:

```
[2015-10-17 07:46:27,508][INFO ][transport                 ]
[Witchfire] Using [org.elasticsearch.shield.transport.
ShieldServerTransportService] as transport service, overridden by
[shield]
[2015-10-17 07:46:27,510][INFO ][transport                 ]
[Witchfire] Using [org.elasticsearch.shield.transport.netty.
ShieldNettyTransport] as transport, overridden by [shield]
[2015-10-17 07:46:27,511][INFO ][http                      ]
[Witchfire] Using [org.elasticsearch.shield.transport.netty.
ShieldNettyHttpServerTransport] as http transport, overridden by
[shield]
```

Once the shield plugin is added, your access to Elasticsearch at `http://localhost:9200` is restricted without a valid authentication.

Adding users and roles

You need to add users and roles in shield to access Elasticsearch. The following simple command can help you add users with a role, and you can set a password for each user:

```
bin/shield/esusers useradd es_admin -r admin
```

Adding roles in shield

Once added, you can verify the user through a `list` command, or you can delete users, change the password, and so on.

```
packtpub@saurzcode:/usr/share/elasticsearch/bin/shield$ sudo ./esusers list
es_admin       : admin
packtpub@saurzcode:/usr/share/elasticsearch/bin/shield$ sudo ./esusers userdel es_admin
packtpub@saurzcode:/usr/share/elasticsearch/bin/shield$ sudo ./esusers list
No users found
```

Listing and removing roles in shield

Please note that the license plugin that we installed enables the 30 day trial version of shield, beyond which it is degraded to limited functionalities and the license needs to be purchased to enable full functionality.

Using Kibana4 on shield protected Elasticsearch

If we need to use Kibana on top of Elasticsearch that is now protected using shield, we need to add a `kibana4-server` role in shield, and provide a corresponding configuration in the Kibana configuration file in the Kibana installation at `config/kibana.yml`.

The following is the Kibana server role:

```
esusers useradd kibana4-server -r kibana4_server -p password
```

The following is the Kibana configuration:

```
kibana_elasticsearch_username: kibana4-server
kibana_elasticsearch_password: password
```

Marvel to monitor

Marvel is a product that helps monitor an Elasticsearch cluster. It provides a single interface to view aggregated analytics on the cluster. You can view the essential metrics for your cluster, such as health, state of nodes, and indices. Marvel can help perform a root cause analysis of cluster-related issues so that you can anticipate problems before they occur and fix them. You can also analyze historical or real-time data with it.

> Marvel 2.0, supporting Elasticsearch 2.0, is a complete rewrite as a Kibana plugin. It is free for use by everyone, but multicluster support comes as a commercial feature. More on Marvel 2.0 can be found here https://www.elastic.co/guide/en/marvel/current/index.html.

Marvel installation

Just like shield, the Marvel installation is also a one step process. We need to execute the following command from the Elasticsearch installation directory:

```
bin/plugin -i elasticsearch/marvel/latest
```

```
packtpub@saurzcode:/usr/share/elasticsearch/bin$ sudo ./plugin -i elasticsearch/marvel/latest
[sudo] password for packtpub:
-> Installing elasticsearch/marvel/latest...
Trying http://download.elasticsearch.org/elasticsearch/marvel/marvel-latest.zip...
Downloading ...........................................................................
..........................................................................................
..........................................................................................
..........................................................................................
..........................................................................................
..........................................................................................
..........................................................................................
.....................................................................DONE
Installed elasticsearch/marvel/latest into /usr/share/elasticsearch/plugins/marvel
```

Marvel installation

The following are some of the features that Marvel provides.

Marvel dashboards

Looking quite similar to Kibana dashboards, Marvel dashboard gives you various metrics about your Elasticsearch cluster, and various nodes and indices. Values in *yellow* need your attention and have to be taken care of.

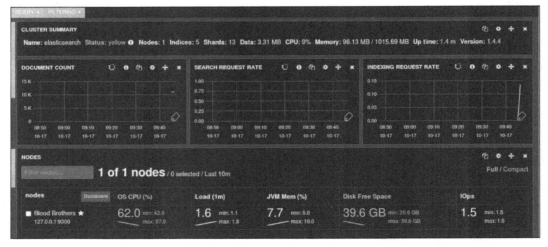

Marvel dashboard

It gives you the **DOCUMENT COUNT, SEARCH REQUEST RATE, INDEXING REQUEST RATE,** various statistics on nodes and indexes, such as **OS CPU, Load, JVM Mem, Disk Free Space** and **IOps** operations, as shown in the following screenshots:

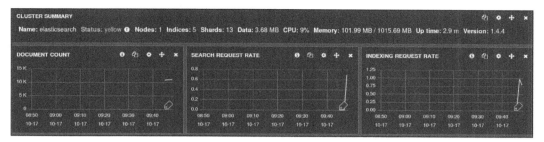

Marvel dashboard statistics

Marvel node metrics

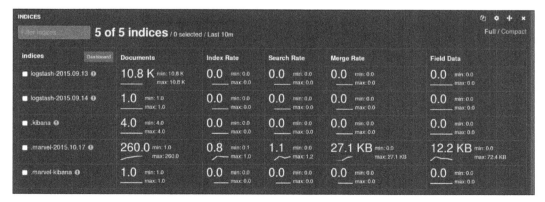

Marvel indices metrics

There is also a very good dashboard that represents the Shard Allocation in your cluster, and where different indices sit on various shards and replicas. It displays all primary nodes and replica nodes with different color codes along with the state of various nodes.

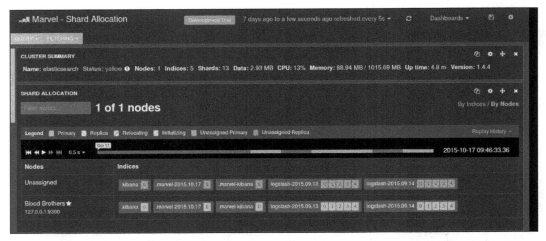

Marvel Shard Allocation dashboard

ELK roadmap

All the tools in ELK Stack and its ecosystem are in an active development phase, and new updates are being pushed regularly. It's evolving rapidly to suit the needs of modern enterprise applications.

Elasticsearch roadmap

Elasticsearch is widely used across companies in various use cases, and its ecosystem and plugins are evolving very rapidly. With a wide range of plugins available for various tasks involving Elasticsearch, it is becoming more and more adaptable to a variety of use cases.

 All plugins and integrations are documented here:

https://www.elastic.co/guide/en/elasticsearch/
plugins/current/index.html

Logstash roadmap

Logstash is probably the most active development among ELK Stack tools. The development team and community are working hard to make the tool more enterprise grade by adding more resiliency, robustness, and maintainability features.

Logstash 1.5.x has already made significant changes related to plugin management and development. The following are the capabilities being added in coming versions of Logstash.

Event persistence capability

Currently we need to use a message broker, such as Redis, and so on, to throttle the event queue or to save losing the events in the pipeline. The upcoming versions of Logstash are going to add the capability of persisting the events queue to disk to avoid loss of data in case of plugin crash or restart.

End-to-end message acknowledgement

The current Logstash implementation lacks the capability of acknowledging the message across end-to-end systems. The upcoming versions of Logstash are planned to include notification of failed events, and so on, so that events can be replayed or handled.

Logstash monitoring and management API

The Logstash process currently lacks the support to monitor the installation, and to track event successes and failures, in the pipeline. Monitoring API planned in future releases is aimed at providing these capabilities.

Also, currently, if you need to change any configuration, you need to change the Logstash configuration file, and the system needs a restart to take the change in to effect. The Logstash management API is planned to overcome this limitation so that configuration can be updated dynamically without interrupting the pipeline.

 More capabilities that are being added to Logstash can be tracked at https://github.com/elastic/logstash/labels/roadmap.

Kibana roadmap

Kibana is getting more and more useful with a variety of use cases now utilizing the tool with ELK Stack, and also the integration with many other systems. With increasing use of analysis on a variety of data, new chart types, and aggregations are being added. The following are some of the recent capabilities added to the platform in version 4.1:

- The ability to build a bubble chart, derived from **Line chart**
- Field formatting options in **Settings**.
- Kibana objects (dashboards, charts and searches) can now be imported and exported as well.

 You can track more new enhancements in Kibana here
https://www.elastic.co/guide/en/kibana/
current/whats-new.html.

Summary

In this chapter, we saw some of the tools and utilities that make your life easy while using ELK Stack. Also, we explored how ELK Stack and its ecosystem are evolving to the needs of modern enterprises to extend its support to multiple systems and data sources.

Index

A

absolute time filter 111
access logs
  grok pattern 137, 139
Advanced Message Queuing Protocol
    (AMQP) 63
Apache Kafka
  about 157
  URL 157
Apache Lucene
  about 87
  URL 87
area chart 126

B

bar chart
  building 36, 37
Bigdesk plugin
  about 103
  URL 103
buckets
  about 121
  Advanced options 125, 126
  aggregations 121
  Date Histogram 122
  Date Range 122
  Histogram 122
  Range 122
  Terms 122
bundler
  URL 84

C

cluster, Elasticsearch
  about 89
  health parameters 94
  health status, checking 93
codec plugins
  about 70
  decode method 80
  encode method 80
  json 70
  line 71
  multiline 71
  plain 72
  plugin methods 80
  register method 80
  rubydebug 72
  URL 72
configuration, Elasticsearch
  cluster name 11
  network address 10
  node name 11
  paths, specifying 10
csv filter
  about 65
  configuration options 65
csv plugin
  about 57
  configuration options 57
Curator
  commands 168
  installation 168, 169
  URL 169
  used, for index management 167, 168

Thank you for buying
Learning ELK Stack

About Packt Publishing

Packt, pronounced 'packed', published its first book, *Mastering phpMyAdmin for Effective MySQL Management*, in April 2004, and subsequently continued to specialize in publishing highly focused books on specific technologies and solutions.

Our books and publications share the experiences of your fellow IT professionals in adapting and customizing today's systems, applications, and frameworks. Our solution-based books give you the knowledge and power to customize the software and technologies you're using to get the job done. Packt books are more specific and less general than the IT books you have seen in the past. Our unique business model allows us to bring you more focused information, giving you more of what you need to know, and less of what you don't.

Packt is a modern yet unique publishing company that focuses on producing quality, cutting-edge books for communities of developers, administrators, and newbies alike. For more information, please visit our website at www.packtpub.com.

About Packt Open Source

In 2010, Packt launched two new brands, Packt Open Source and Packt Enterprise, in order to continue its focus on specialization. This book is part of the Packt Open Source brand, home to books published on software built around open source licenses, and offering information to anybody from advanced developers to budding web designers. The Open Source brand also runs Packt's Open Source Royalty Scheme, by which Packt gives a royalty to each open source project about whose software a book is sold.

Writing for Packt

We welcome all inquiries from people who are interested in authoring. Book proposals should be sent to author@packtpub.com. If your book idea is still at an early stage and you would like to discuss it first before writing a formal book proposal, then please contact us; one of our commissioning editors will get in touch with you.

We're not just looking for published authors; if you have strong technical skills but no writing experience, our experienced editors can help you develop a writing career, or simply get some additional reward for your expertise.

[PACKT] open source
community experience distilled
PUBLISHING

Elasticsearch
Blueprints

A practical project-based guide to generating compelling search
solutions using the dynamic and powerful features of Elasticsearch

Vineeth Mohan   [PACKT] open source

Elasticsearch Blueprints

ISBN: 978-1-78398-492-3   Paperback: 192 pages

A practical project-based guide to generating
compelling search solutions using the dynamic and
powerful features of Elasticsearch

1. Discover the power of Elasticsearch by
    implementing it in a variety of real-world
    scenarios such as restaurant and
    e-commerce search.

2. Discover how the features you see in an
    average Google search can be achieved
    using Elasticsearch.

3. Learn how to not only generate accurate search
    results, but also improve the quality of searches
    for relevant results.

Building a Search Server
with Elasticsearch
Daniel Beach

[PACKT] VIDEO

Building a Search Server with Elasticsearch [Video]

ISBN: 978-1-78328-415-3   Duration: 01:53 hrs

Build a fully featured and scalable search UI with
Elasticsearch

1. Start building your own search engine
    with Elasticsearch, from setup to ingestion
    and querying.

2. Set up an Elasticsearch cluster and a full
    search interface in AngularJS, all in one
    comprehensive project.

3. Implement search features such as highlighting,
    filters, and autocomplete, and build a robust
    search engine.

Please check **www.PacktPub.com** for information on our titles

Mastering Elasticsearch
Second Edition

ISBN: 978-1-78355-379-2   Paperback: 434 pages

Further your knowledge of the Elasticsearch server by learning more about its internals, querying, and data handling

1. Understand Apache Lucene and Elasticsearch's design and architecture.

2. Design your index, configure it, and distribute it, not only with assumptions, but with the underlying knowledge of how it works.

3. Improve your user search experience with Elasticsearch functionality and learn how to develop your own Elasticsearch plugins.

ElasticSearch Cookbook
Second Edition

ISBN: 978-1-78355-483-6   Paperback: 472 pages

Over 130 advanced recipes to search, analyze, deploy, manage, and monitor data effectively with ElasticSearch

1. Deploy and manage simple ElasticSearch nodes as well as complex cluster topologies.

2. Write native plugins to extend the functionalities of ElasticSearch to boost your business.

3. Packed with clear, step-by-step recipes to walk you through the capabilities of ElasticSearch.

Please check **www.PacktPub.com** for information on our titles